THE CLEAR AND PRESENT TRUTH OF THE 2300, 1260, 1290, AND 1335-DAY PROPHECIES

Rapid Movements Publishing
Hampton, GA 30228

Copyright © 2021 by Tory St.Cyr

Printed in the United States of America
All Rights Reserved

Published by Rapid Movements Publishing
Hampton, GA 30228

Other books by Tory St.Cyr may be purchased at www.clearandpresenttruth.com

The author assumes full responsibility for the accuracy of all facts and quotations, as cited in this book.

ISBN: 978-1-7366073-2-9

Pictures and Illustrations by Goodsalt.com and Freepik.com

This book is dedicated to those of us who have studied the time-based prophecies of Daniel. God answers prayer.

Contents

Preface 9
Time-Based Prophecies 101 11
How Long? 19
The 2300-Day Prophecy 23
The 1260-Day Prophecy 65
The Answer to "How Long" 89
The 1290-Day Prophecy 97
The 1335-Day Prophecy 111
Test Your Knowledge 129
Answers 133
Topical Index 137

Preface

I can still remember reading Daniel 12 for the first time. My eyes lit up with intrigue when I discovered the 1290 and 1335-day prophecies. I was familiar with the 2300-day, the 70-weeks, and the 1260-day prophecies; however, these additional prophecies felt like a hidden code in a video game. What was the meaning of these timeframes?

I assumed someone somewhere had written a book on these time prophecies, and I would be able to explain their meaning when the situation called for it. However, the day came when someone asked me about these prophecies, and I didn't have an answer. I decided to ask someone but still didn't feel confident in their response. That's when I decided to do my own research. I prayed that God would help me make sense of these prophecies, and I truly believe that's what He did.

Once you read this book, you will realize that these time-based prophecies can all be understood through prayer and the power of the Holy Spirit.

You may not agree with everything I've written in this book; however, I hope you can at least understand how my conclusions were made. I truly believe God is coming soon, and He desires that our understanding of these time-based prophecies is correct.

I pray that God will use this book to richly bless anyone who reads its pages. And as with all my books, keep a watchful eye, but also have an open and willing heart.

Chapter 1

Time-Based Prophecies 101

Of all the mysteries in the Word of God, time-based prophecies are at the top of my list for most difficult to understand. When I say "time-based prophecies," I'm not referring to the occasion when Jonah told the Ninevites that they would be destroyed in 40 days. I'm also not referring to that instance when the prophet Isaiah told King Hezekiah that God had given him another 15 years to live. These time prophecies are amazing, but they are not mysterious. We understand when those prophecies began, and we know what the fulfillment of those prophecies entailed. The time-based prophecies that I've found to be the most mysterious are the ones found in the Book of Daniel.

As a young man, I can remember reading through the Book of Daniel and stumbling upon various time prophecies that were so mysterious that I never even attempted to understand what they meant. However, here I am, twenty years later, actually writing a book on the very prophecies that intimidated me like a school bully after the final bell.

If you are like me, you may have read these time-based prophecies and decided that it was simply too early in the morning to even attempt figuring out what these time periods meant. Then later that evening, you open the Bible and realize that it's too close to your bedtime to utilize so much brainpower. And then the next thing you know, it's twenty years later, and you still have no idea what these prophecies mean.

Let me get to my point before I have to rename this chapter "My Life's Regrets." My point is, there are certain prophecies in the Book of Daniel that I've always avoided until now. I got to the point where I no longer felt content with only a surface knowledge of these prophecies. I started feeling like God wanted me to dig deeper—and that's what we are about to do.

There are four time-based prophecies in the Book of Daniel that deserve our attention: The 2300-day prophecy, the 1290-day prophecy, the 1260-day prophecy, and the 1335-day prophecy. We will go deeper into these prophecies, but before we do that, let's list the scriptures that contain the above-listed prophecies:

> And he said unto me, Unto **two thousand and three hundred days**; then shall the sanctuary be cleansed. Daniel 8:14

> And I heard the man clothed in linen, which was upon the waters of the river, when he held up his right hand and his left hand unto heaven, and sware by him that liveth for ever that it shall be for a **time, times, and an half**; and when he shall have accomplished to scatter the power of

the holy people, all these things shall be finished. Daniel 12:7 (Later, we will see how this is calculated as 1260 days)

And from the time that the daily sacrifice shall be taken away, and the abomination that maketh desolate set up, there shall be a **thousand two hundred and ninety days**. Daniel 12:11

Blessed is he that waiteth, and cometh to the **thousand three hundred and five and thirty days**. Daniel 12:12

And there you have it. Four scriptures and four different time-based prophecies.

Before we decipher the meaning of these scriptures, we need to lay some basic ground rules regarding time prophecy:

1. **Time prophecies will never give us the day and hour of the Second Coming.**

Regarding the Second Coming, Jesus made it clear when He said, "*But of that day and that hour knoweth no man, no, not the angels which are in heaven, neither the Son, but the Father.*" Mark 13:32

This scripture makes it plain that time-based prophecies will never give us the day and hour of Jesus' return. If you are being told that there is a prophecy in the Bible that informs us when Jesus is coming back, you should know he or she is misinterpreting scripture, or worse, trying to deceive you. In either case, you are dealing with error.

2. A day is often calculated as a year in Bible prophecy.

There is a Biblical principle called the day-for-a-year principle. Notice how the Bible presents this concept:

> After the number of the days in which ye searched the land, even forty days, **each day for a year**, shall ye bear your iniquities, even forty years, and ye shall know my breach of promise. Numbers 14:34

> And when thou hast accomplished them, lie again on thy right side, and thou shalt bear the iniquity of the house of Judah forty days: I have appointed thee each **day for a year**. Ezekiel 4:6

Not every time-based prophecy adheres to this principle. However, according to the Scriptures, certain time-based prophecies are calculated by converting each day to a year.

3. A prophetic year is 360 days.

A prophetic year consists of 360 literal days.[1] It is important to understand this fact, as some of our modern-day calendars have 365 days with leap years.

---

[1] Riley, J. W.. The World's Empire. United States: Journal Company, 1873. P. 72

There is evidence that may suggest ancient calendars also consisted of 360-day years. In the book of Genesis, we find that five months consisted of 150 days:

> "In the six hundredth year of Noah's life, in the **second month**, the seventeenth day of the month, the same day were all the fountains of the great deep broken up, and the windows of heaven were opened." Genesis 7:11

Notice when the waters subsided:

> "And the ark rested in the **seventh month**, on the seventeenth day of the month, upon the mountains of Ararat." Genesis 8:4

Notice how Genesis breaks down this five-month period into days:

> "And the waters prevailed upon the earth an **hundred and fifty days**." Genesis 7:24

It should be clear that Genesis calculated five months as 150 days. This may be an indication that ancient times consisted of 360-day years (twelve months of 30 days).

Also, from a practical standpoint, it makes sense that the prophetic year was calculated using a 360-day static year. Can you imagine if every prophecy had to be calculated with some months consisting of 30 days and other months consisting of 31 days? Then we would have to decipher which calendar applies to the prophecy— The Julian, Gregorian, or the Hebrew. In His wisdom, it would appear God kept the time-based prophecies simple by giving us a standard 30-month, 360-day criteria for time.

4. Years are counted backward in the BC era.

In these modern times, our calendar years numerically advance. For example, it is currently 2021; next year, it will be 2022. However, if this were the BC era, next year would be 2020, as we would be counting in reverse.

I'm not a mathematician, but a simple way to think of the BC to AD transition is similar to a positive/negative graph.

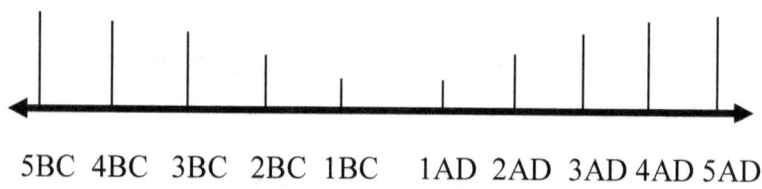

5BC 4BC 3BC 2BC 1BC   1AD 2AD 3AD 4AD 5AD

Notice the years numerically decrease until they get to year 1BC; then they numerically increase from that point forward. Also, notice there is no year zero.

The BC to AD transition is important because some of Daniel's time-based prophecies begin in BC and end in AD. If we don't understand how to count BC years, then our calculation of prophecy will become distorted.

Also, I want you to be aware that those who lived during Old Testament times did not actually count their years backward. They appear to have calculated their years by the reign of their rulers. Here's an example:

> "In the **second year of Joash** son of Jehoahaz king of Israel reigned Amaziah the son of Joash king of Judah." 2King 14:1

Well, if the people living in ancient times kept track of time by the reign of their kings, how and when did we begin this BC to AD dating system? In my research, I discovered that in 525 AD, a Scythian monk named Dionysius Exiguus devised a dating system that labeled the era before Christ as BC and the era during Christ and afterward as AD (Anno Domini, a Latin phrase meaning: The year of our Lord). Unfortunately, Dionysius miscalculated the birth of Christ,[2] and so it should be understood that Jesus was probably born sometime around 4 BC.

Now, before we move to the next chapter, let's recap what we've learned in this chapter:

- This book will focus on four time-based prophecies.
- The four prophecies we are looking at are the 2300-day prophecy, the 1260-day prophecy, the 1290-day prophecy, and the 1335-day prophecy.
- None of these prophecies are intended to give us the day or hour of the Second Coming.

---

[2] Britannica, The Editors of Encyclopaedia. "Dionysius Exiguus". Encyclopedia Britannica, 23 Apr. 2013, https://www.britannica.com/biography/Dionysius-Exiguus. Accessed 27 March 2021.

- It may be appropriate to apply the day-for-a-year principle to these prophecies.
- These prophetic years are comprised of 360 literal days.
- The years in BC count backward.

Now that you've graduated from my time-based prophecies 101 course (I hope it was everything you dreamed it would be), you should now feel invigorated and empowered knowing that you are well equipped for what's about to come.

I know you may be questioning what exactly is about to come; however, our focus shouldn't be on what's coming....our focus should be on—How Long?

Chapter 2

How Long?

Daniel had visions and dreams. On one occasion, Daniel's vision allowed him to witness a conversation between two angels. The conversation was short but powerful. Here is what was said:

> "Then I heard one saint speaking, and another saint said unto that certain saint which spake, How long shall be the vision concerning the daily sacrifice, and the transgression of desolation, to give both the sanctuary and the host to be trodden under foot?" Daniel 8:13

I want you to notice that a question was asked. The question began with the phrase—How long. But notice this question is really two questions phrased as one question.

1. How long is the vision concerning the Daily Sacrifice and the Transgression of Desolation?
2. How long will both the sanctuary and the host be trodden under foot?

Notice the angel's response:

> "And he said unto me, Unto two thousand and three hundred days; then shall the sanctuary be cleansed." Daniel 8:14

Are you seeing this? Do you see anything out of the ordinary regarding this conversation? I do.

Let's unpack this question. However, before we do this, I want you to understand we are not unpacking it as Bible scholars; we are unpacking this conversation as everyday people overhearing a conversation. Tell me—What is different about this conversation?

Let's simply observe what just happened. Two angels were talking, and one angel said to the other angel—How long is the vision concerning the Daily Sacrifice, and how long is the vision concerning the Transgression (also known as the Abomination) of Desolation?

The first thing I want you to notice is that the angel who was asked the question never responded to the inquiring angel. The scripture says, "*And he said unto ME.*" Let me ask you something: How often does someone ask you a question, and you look at someone else and give that person an answer instead of the individual who asked the question?

You may find this interaction completely normal, but I believe there is more happening here than we realize. Now, let's analyze the angel's answer to the question:

The angel answers and says, "*Unto two thousand and three hundred days; then shall the sanctuary be cleansed.*"

You may not see it at this moment, and you may disagree when I reveal it to you, but it is clear to me that the angel did not answer the question that he was asked. Think about the question: "How long will the vision concerning the Daily Sacrifice and the Abomination of Desolation last?" Notice, the angel was not asked how long it would take for the sanctuary to be cleansed, yet that is the answer he gave to Daniel. So, we have two "irregularities."

1. The angel does not respond to the inquiring angel but instead responds to Daniel.
2. The angel answers a question that was not asked of him.

I'm not suggesting that the angel ignored the question; I'm simply suggesting that the answer is given a little later. Ladies and Gentlemen, buckle up because you are about to see that this conversation between Daniel and the two angels is the foundation of the 2300, the 1260, the 1290, and the 1335-day prophecies.

Now, let's take a look at the 2300-day prophecy.

Chapter 3

The 2300-Day Prophecy

> *"And he said unto me, Unto two thousand and three hundred days; then shall the sanctuary be cleansed."* Daniel 8:14

The 2300-day prophecy is an important truth for these last days. While this prophecy may be complex to many, remember the Spirit of Truth was sent into the world to give us understanding.

In order for us to understand the 2300-day prophecy, we must answer four questions:

1. What is the sanctuary?
2. What does it mean to cleanse the sanctuary?
3. When was the sanctuary cleansed?
4. Is there a New Covenant Sanctuary?

Let's begin.

What is the sanctuary?

Regarding the physical structure, the author of Hebrews gives us a good description:

> "Then indeed, even the first covenant had ordinances of divine service and the

earthly sanctuary. For a tabernacle was prepared: the first part [The Holy Place], in which was the lampstand, the table, and the showbread [table of show-bread], which is called the sanctuary; and behind the second veil, the part of the tabernacle which is called the Holiest of All [The Most Holy Place], which had the golden censer [Altar of incense] and the ark of the covenant overlaid on all sides with gold, in which were the golden pot that had the manna, Aaron's rod that budded, and the tablets of the covenant; and above it were the cherubim of glory overshadowing the mercy seat. Of these things we cannot now speak in detail." Hebrews 9:1-5 NKJV

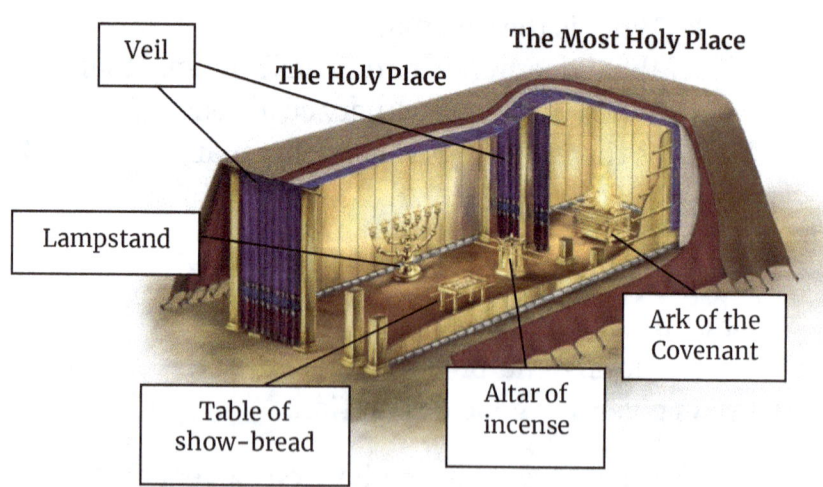

In the Bible, we find God instructing Moses with these words:

> "And let them make me a sanctuary; that I may dwell among them." Exodus 25:8

Simply put, God wanted the Children of Israel to have a symbol of His presence as they wandered through the desert. In this way, God was able to be with His people. However, the sanctuary was more than God's way of dwelling with his people; it was also how God dealt with Israel's sins. Notice how the Bible conveys this thought:

> "For the bodies of those beasts, whose blood is brought into the **sanctuary** by the high priest **for sin**, are burned without the camp." Hebrews 13:11

It should be clear from the above Scripture that the purpose of the sanctuary was for God to dwell with His people and deal with their sins.

What is the Cleansing of the Sanctuary?

In order to understand the Cleansing of the Sanctuary, we must understand the ministration of the sanctuary. Regarding this ministration, the Bible says,

> "And almost all things are by the law purged with blood; and without shedding of blood is no remission." Hebrews 9:22

According to the Bible, the only way God pardoned

sin is through the shedding of blood. Notice how the Bible describes the work of the sanctuary and how the shedding of blood was performed by the priest:

> "And he shall lay his hand upon the head of the goat, and kill it in the place where they kill the burnt offering before the LORD: it is a sin offering." Leviticus 4:24

Prior to the sacrifice, the sinner placed his hand *upon the head of the goat.* As a matter of fact, almost every sacrificial offering followed this protocol. However, we must ask ourselves—Why would the sinner need to place his hand upon the head of the goat? The answer is found in Leviticus:

> And Aaron shall lay both his hands upon the head of the live goat, and **confess over him all the iniquities of the children of Israel**... Leviticus 16:21

When the Children of Israel performed the sin offering, they placed their hands on the head of the goat and confessed their sins. Then they killed the goat.

It is important to understand this sequence of events. Romans 6:23 tells us, *"The wages of sin is death."* If the wages of sin is death, then sinners under the Old Covenant should have been killed for their sins. However, we see that once they confessed over the head of the goat, the goat received sin's wages, not the sinner. This reveals what was happening while the sins were being confessed over the head of the goat. When the sinner placed his hand on the head of that goat and confessed his sins, he symbolically transferred his sins to the goat. This is why the goat received the sentence that the sinner deserved, even though the goat was innocent.

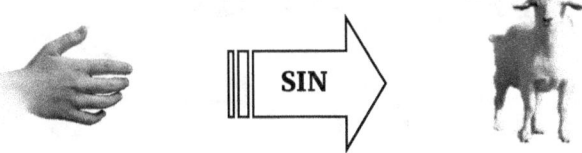

We also must be aware that the sacrificial process did not end once the goat was killed. The Bible tells us what happened next:

> "And the priest shall take of the blood of the sin offering with his finger, and put it upon the horns of the altar of burnt offering, and shall pour out his blood at the bottom of the altar of burnt offering." Leviticus 4:25

Are you seeing this? Once the goat was sacrificed, his blood was carried into the sanctuary! The question is—Why would God command his blood to be brought into the sanctuary? If we think about the sequence of events, we can see what is happening.

The sinner symbolically transferred his sins to the animal. Then the animal was killed.

If the sinner symbolically transferred his sins to the animal by confessing over it, then what do you think happened when the priest carried the blood of the slain animal into the sanctuary?

Ladies and Gentlemen, when the priest carried the blood into the Holy Place, he symbolically transferred the sin to the sanctuary!

The thought of sin being transferred to God's sanctuary may sound insane to many of you, but later I believe you will see that the Bible supports this idea.

Please understand that this sacrificial work that allowed Israel's sins to be transferred from the sinner to the sanctuary occurred on a daily basis. Hebrews confirms this daily work with the following words:

> "Who needeth not **daily**, as those high priests, to offer up sacrifice, first for his own sins, and then for the people's: for this he did once..." Hebrews 7:27

Day by day throughout the year, the sins of Israel were transferred to the sanctuary. However, those sins did not remain in the sanctuary. According to Scripture, God established a yearly ceremony to have those sins removed from the sanctuary. Notice how the Bible conveys this thought:

> "But into the second went the high priest alone **once every year**, not without blood, which he offered for himself, and for the errors of the people." Hebrews 9:7

This once-a-year ceremony was known as Yom Kippur or the Day of Atonement; however, Daniel called it the Cleansing of the Sanctuary! The literal translation of 'kippurim' is cleansing.[3] According to Jewish tradition, God inscribed each person's fate for the coming year into the Book of Life and waited until Yom Kippur to "seal" the verdict.[4]

We see this special service in Leviticus 16. Notice how the chapter conveys this cleansing ceremony:

> "And he shall make **an atonement for the holy place**, because of the uncleanness of the children of Israel, and because of their transgressions in all their sins..." Leviticus 16:16

Atonement in the original language can mean to disannul, forgive, pardon, purge, or cleanse. This once-

---

[3] "Yom Kippur: the meaning of its name". Texas Jewish Post. 2020-09-24. Retrieved 2021-01-16.
[4] "Yom Kippur Theology and Themes". My Jewish Learning. Retrieved September 27, 2020.

a-year ceremony, known as the Day of Atonement, involved a sacrifice similar to the daily sacrifice, but there were key differences. Here is what occurred during this special service:

1. On the Day of Atonement, two goats were brought to the door of the tabernacle (Leviticus 16:7).

2. One goat was determined to be for the Lord, and the other goat was determined to be the scapegoat (Leviticus 16:8).

3. The Lord's goat was then sacrificed by the high priest (Leviticus 16:9).

4. After the goat of the sin offering was killed, the high priest brought *the blood within the vail...and sprinkled it upon the mercy seat, and before the mercy seat* (Leviticus 16:15).

5. During this service, the Children of Israel were commanded to afflict[5] themselves (Leviticus 23:27).

6. If the Children of Israel did not afflict their souls, they were cut off from among the people that same day (Leviticus 23:29).

7. After an atonement was made for the sanctuary and the people, the high priest placed both hands on the head of the scapegoat and confessed over him the iniquities, transgressions, and sins of the Children of Israel. This transferred the sins from

---

[5] Humble oneself, chasten self, or submitting self. This involved spending the day in solemn humiliation before God, with prayer, fasting, and deep searching of heart.

the sanctuary onto the scapegoat. (Leviticus 16:20-21).

8. Finally, the goat which carried all the transferred sins was sent away into an uninhabited land, never to return. (Leviticus 16:21-22).

The word cleansing in the original language means to justify. This justification of the sanctuary was a work of judgment, pardon, and a work designed for Israel to see their Redeemer by faith.

When was the sanctuary to be cleansed?
We've established the role of the sanctuary. We've also discovered that the sanctuary went through a ceremony to cleanse it. Now we must determine when the Cleansing of the Sanctuary began.

Remember, Daniel 8:14 says, "*Unto two thousand and three hundred days; then shall the sanctuary be cleansed.*" This scripture tells us the prophecy's duration but doesn't tell us when the 2300 days began. As a matter of fact, this whole chapter doesn't appear to address the prophecy's starting point. If the Prophet Daniel addressed a starting point and it's not in chapter 8, it must be in a different chapter.

In Daniel 9, we see the prophet praying to the Lord. In the middle of his prayer, the angel returns. Notice what the angel tells Daniel:

> "And he informed me, and talked with me, and said, O Daniel, I am now come forth to give thee skill and understanding." Daniel 9:22

The angel came back to give Daniel skill and understanding. The question is—understanding of what? If you read the end of chapter 8, you will see that even though Daniel received the vision, he didn't understand everything he saw.

> "I was astounded at the vision, and there was no one who could explain it."
> Daniel 8:27 AMP

It appears that the angel came back to give Daniel an understanding of the vision that was recorded in chapter 8. However, when the angel begins giving Daniel the explanation, he mentions another time prophecy!

The 70-Weeks Prophecy

> "Seventy weeks are determined upon thy people and upon thy holy city, to finish the transgression, and to make an end of sins, and to make reconciliation for iniquity, and to bring in everlasting righteousness, and to seal up the vision and prophecy, and to anoint the most Holy." Daniel 9:24

While the angel came to give Daniel understanding, he revealed to the prophet that 70 weeks were determined upon his people and upon his holy city. Determined in the original language means "to cut" or "to divide."[6] The King James translators believed the

---

[6] "H2852 - ḥāṯak - Strong's Hebrew Lexicon (KJV)." Blue Letter Bible. Accessed 6 Apr, 2021. https://www.blueletterbible.org//lang/lexicon/lexicon.cfm?Strongs=H2852&t=KJV

word "determined" fit the context, but in reality, the angel was telling Daniel that 70 weeks were "cut out" for his people and his holy city. If 70 weeks were cut out for the Children of Israel, we must ask ourselves the question—From what were the 70 weeks cut out? Clearly, the 70 weeks had to be cut out of a larger timeframe.

If you think about this in monetary terms, it equates to you having $70 and someone telling you to "cut out" $100 from the $70. Mathematically, this is impossible. The only way to cut out $100 is if you have $100 or more. The same is true of the cutting-out of the 70 weeks—it had to be cut from a larger timeframe. And since we've established a connection between Daniel 8 and Daniel 9, we should see that the 2300-day prophecy is that larger timeframe. Ladies and Gentlemen, if the 70 weeks were cut out of the 2300-days, then this reveals to us that the 2300-day prophecy and the 70-weeks prophecy had the same starting point!

Hopefully, I haven't caused you to become sidetracked. Remember, we are trying to determine when the sanctuary was cleansed. Daniel 9 revealed that the starting point for the 2300-day prophecy was the same starting point for the 70-weeks prophecy. Now, all we need to do is determine when the 70 weeks began.

The 70 weeks compute to 490 days (70 x 7). Utilizing the day-for-a-year principle established in this book's first chapter, we confirm that the 70 weeks are 490 literal years. This 490-year period was how much time was determined for the Children of Israel and the holy city to meet the standards of Jehovah. However, knowing the duration of the 70-weeks prophecy still leaves one glaring question: What is the starting point for the 70-weeks prophecy?

Thankfully, the angel didn't leave Daniel in suspense regarding the starting point of the prophecy. The messenger solemnly made this declaration to the prophet:

> "Know therefore and understand, that **from the going forth of the commandment to restore and to build Jerusalem** unto the Messiah the Prince shall be seven weeks, and threescore and two weeks..." Daniel 9:25

Please notice that the command was not just to build Jerusalem; the command was also to *restore* Jerusalem.

Jerusalem needed to be restored and rebuilt because King Nebuchadnezzar destroyed the holy city between 587-586 BC. The angel here revealed to Daniel that there would be a restoration of the city and that the command for this restoration would be the starting point for the 70-weeks prophecy.

Now that we understand what event began the 70-weeks prophecy, all we need to do now is determine when the command to restore and build Jerusalem went into effect.

In the book of Ezra, we discover that there are a total of three commands to build Jerusalem. However, only one of those decrees was to *restore and build* Jerusalem. In Ezra 7, we find the only command to *restore* Jerusalem's civil government, its religious customs, and *build* the temple. This decree was given in 457 BC.[7]

The 70-weeks prophecy goes on to reveal when the Messiah would get baptized, when He would die, and when the gospel would go to the Gentiles as a result of the Jews losing their favored status.

Remember, this chapter's focus is the 2300-day prophecy, not the 70-weeks prophecy; however, in order to understand the starting point for the 2300-day prophecy, we needed to broach the subject of the 70-weeks. Now that we know the starting point of the 2300 days, we can determine the date for the Cleansing of the Sanctuary.

Before we move further, let's make sure we are all on the same page (no pun intended) by reviewing this chapter's highlights thus far:

1. In Daniel 8, the angel declared to Daniel that the sanctuary would be cleansed after 2300 years.

2. Daniel did not understand the vision; therefore, the angel returned in Daniel 9 to give him an understanding.

3. The angel revealed a 70-week time prophecy, but this time a starting point was given.

4. The starting point was the command to restore and build Jerusalem, which was given in 457 BC.

---

[7] Milligan, Robert. Reason and Revelation: Or, The Province of Reason in Matters Pertaining to Divine Revelation Defined and Illustrated, and the Paramount Authority of the Holy Scriptures Vindicated. United States: R. W. Carroll, 1868.

5. It has been determined that the 70-weeks prophecy and the 2300-day prophecy are connected and thus began at the same point in history.

Now that we understand when the 2300 days began, it should be fairly simple to determine when the 2300 days ended and the sanctuary cleansed. I'm a visual learner, so let's make this into a chart/diagram:

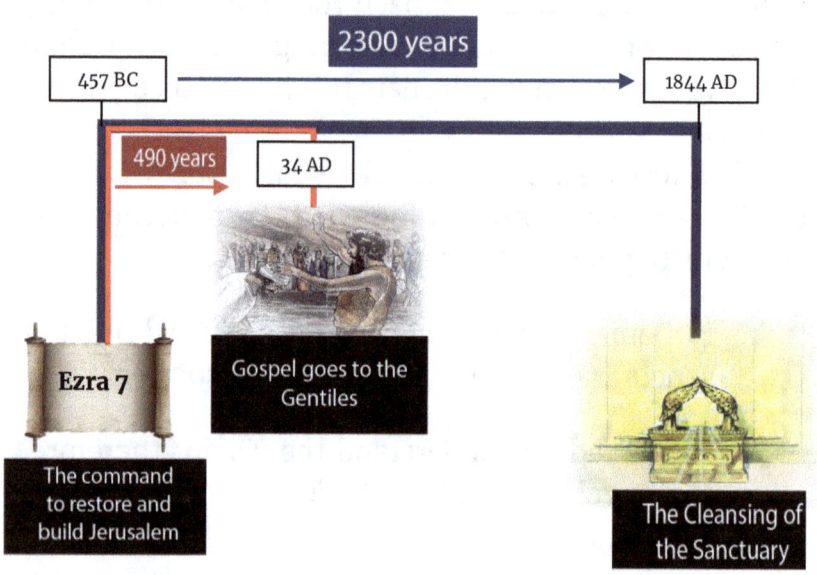

The above chart should help us see how the 490 years were cut from the larger 2300-year period. We can also see that the 2300-year prophecy takes us to the year 1844 AD.

1843 or 1844?

We must understand that 2300 minus 457 equals 1843. This calculation should logically lead us to ask the question—How do we determine the year is 1844 when the math says it should be 1843? We declare 1844 because the command to restore and build Jerusalem didn't fall on the first day of 457 BC; the command began in the autumn of 457 BC when the work to rebuild *the street and the wall* commenced.[8] Therefore, that first year extended unto the autumn of 456 BC. This means that the last year of the 2300-day prophecy fell in 1843 but extended into 1844.

If what I just stated is unclear, I will illustrate how this is calculated utilizing a spreadsheet.

	Year beginning	Year Ending	Year Count
1			
2	-457	-456	1
3	-456	-455	2
4	-455	-454	3
457	-2	-1	456
458	-1	1	457
459	1	2	458
491	33	34	490
492	34	35	491
493	35	36	492
2299	1841	1842	2298
2300	1842	1843	2299
2301	1843	1844	2300
2302	1844	1845	2301
2303			

Because the prophecy began in the autumn of 457 BC, the first year extended to the following year, which was 456 BC.

Notice, I removed the year 0 from this spreadsheet.

As you can see, the 2300th year of the prophecy began in 1843 but extended to the autumn of 1844.

Most rows have been hidden in the above chart.

---

[8] Smith, Uriah. *Daniel and the Revelation*. United Kingdom: Southern Pub. Association, 1907. p. 220

Now that we've determined 1844 was the year the sanctuary was cleansed, we now must determine what day and month of 1844 this prophecy came to a close.

According to Leviticus 16:29, the Day of Atonement always fell on the "*seventh month, on the tenth day of the month*" of the Jewish calendar. The Day of Atonement can vary from year to year but typically falls between September and October of our modern Gregorian calendar.

October 22nd or September 23rd?

To be fair, there is some dispute whether the Day of Atonement in 1844 fell on September 23rd or October 22nd. Behind this dispute is a variation between two Jewish calendars. The source of this calendar variation comes from the fact that Rabbinic Jews changed their method of reckoning the Jewish year, while a different sect, known as the Karaite Jews, believed in the original method of reckoning the Biblical year. As a result of this difference, the Rabbinic Jews would have celebrated Yom Kippur on September 23, 1844, while the Karaite Jews should've celebrated it on October 22, 1844.

While most Karaite Jews eventually adopted the Rabbinic method of reckoning their calendars, I believe the Karaite method is the most accurate; therefore, I conclude the tenth day of the seventh month according to the Jewish calendar fell on October 22, 1844.

With that understanding, we now ask ourselves this question: How could the sanctuary have been cleansed in 1844 when there was no sanctuary in Jerusalem? The answer is clear once we realize there is a New Covenant Sanctuary.

Was there a New Covenant sanctuary?

Have you ever heard the phrase "types and shadows?" I first learned of this phrase when I began reading the works of various Bible scholars. If you are unfamiliar with this phrase or its meaning, I hope the below explanation will provide clarity:

1Corinthians 10:11 says, "*Now all these things happened unto them for **ensamples**: and they are written for our admonition, upon whom the ends of the world are come.*" In the original language, the word for *ensamples* is "*typos,*" which can be defined as a type i.e., a person or thing prefiguring a future (Messianic) person or thing.[9]

Colossians 2:16-17 says, "*Let no man therefore judge you in meat, or in drink, or in respect of an holyday, or of the new moon, or of the sabbath days: Which are a **shadow** of things to come; but the body is of Christ.*" In the original language, the word for *shadow* is "*skia,*" which can be defined as an image cast by an object and representing the form of that object. In other words, depending on the position of the sun, you may see someone's shadow before you see the actual person. And when you see that shadow, you know the real person is right around the corner.

Bible scholars often refer to "*typos*" and "*skia*" as types and shadows. These types and shadows are usually components of the Old Testament that foreshadowed things that would happen in the New Testament.

---

[9] "G5179 - typos - Strong's Greek Lexicon (KJV)." Blue Letter Bible. Accessed 7 Apr, 2021. https://www.blueletterbible.org//lang/lexicon/lexicon.cfm?Strongs=G5179&t=KJV

For example, Jesus said, "*For as Jonas was three days and three nights in the whale's belly; so shall the Son of man be three days and three nights in the heart of the earth*" Matthew 12:40. Here, Jonah represented a *type* of Christ.

In the Old Testament, types and shadows were prevalent, but it seemed like Israel often got caught up in the shadows and ignored the actual fulfillment of those shadows. One of those shadows was the service of the sanctuary, which the Book of Hebrews called *a shadow of good* or *heavenly things*:

> "For the law having **a shadow of good things to come**, and not the very image of the things, can never with those sacrifices which they offered year by year continually make the comers thereunto perfect." Hebrews 10:1

> "...seeing that there are priests that offer gifts according to the law: **Who serve unto the example and shadow of heavenly things**, as Moses was admonished of God when he was about to make the tabernacle..." Hebrews 8:4-5

It should be clear from these scriptures that the law pertaining to sacrifices was a shadow of things to come. In essence, all the sacrifices that occurred in the Old Covenant sanctuary were simply revealing what would happen under the New Covenant.

By now, I hope you are coming to the realization that the tabernacle built by Moses and the temple later built by Solomon were the sanctuaries of the Old Covenant. However, we are under a New Covenant, and what you must understand is that this New Covenant also has a sanctuary! Notice what the Book of Hebrews tells us:

> "Now of the things which we have spoken this is the sum: We have such an high priest, who is set on the right hand of the throne of the Majesty in the heavens; A minister of the sanctuary, and of the **true tabernacle**, which the Lord pitched, and not man." Hebrews 8:1-2

Are you seeing this? The Bible clearly teaches that there is a TRUE TABERNACLE. It's important to understand that this True Tabernacle is the sanctuary of the New Covenant, and this sanctuary was not built by man but by God Himself as a pattern for the earthly sanctuary. Notice what God told Moses when he commanded the sanctuary to be built:

> "Who serve unto the example and shadow of heavenly things, as Moses was admonished of God when he was about to make the tabernacle: for, **See, saith he, that thou make all things according to the pattern shewed to thee in the mount.**" Hebrews 8:5

God's Word is clear; the sanctuaries built by Moses and later by Solomon were simply copies of the original. However, the question now is—Where is the original sanctuary? The Bible tells us:

> "For Christ is not entered into the holy places made with hands, which are the figures of the true; **but into heaven itself**, now to appear in the presence of God for us." Hebrews 9:24

The Bible is clear. *Christ is not entered into holy places made with hands.* It appears the Bible is declaring that there are Holy Places out of this world (literally). However, these Holy Places weren't built by human hands; they were built by the Hand of God. Ladies and Gentlemen, the Bible is revealing to us that there is a Heavenly Sanctuary!

If you aren't sold on this idea, I will share a few scriptures that prove there is a True Sanctuary in heaven with true furniture. Notice John the Revelator saw the seven golden candlesticks in heaven:

> "And out of the throne proceeded lightnings and thunderings and voices: and there were **seven lamps of fire** burning before the throne, which are the seven Spirits of God." Revelation 4:5

John also saw the altar of incense:

> "And another angel came and stood at **the altar**, having a golden censer; and there was given unto him much **incense**, that he should offer it with the prayers

of all saints upon the golden altar which was before the throne." Revelation 8:3

These are components of the Holy Place, which is also called the first compartment of the Sanctuary. However, Scriptures reveal that John the Revelator was also shown the Most Holy Place or the second compartment of the Sanctuary:

> "And the temple of God was opened in heaven, and there was seen in his temple the **ark of his testament**..." Revelation 11:19

In vision, John saw the seven candlesticks, the altar of incense, and the ark of the covenant. John's visions should make it clear that the earthly sanctuary was simply a replica of the True Sanctuary in heaven.

Ladies and Gentlemen, I want you to think about everything that you've read thus far. We've established that there was an earthly sanctuary and a Heavenly Sanctuary; however, we now must show how the activity in the *typical* sanctuary is the same activity that occurs in the True Sanctuary.

The work of the Heavenly Sanctuary

In order to understand the 2300-day prophecy, we must establish the fact that everything that happened in the earthly sanctuary was simply a shadow of what would take place in the Heavenly Sanctuary.

According to Scripture, both sanctuaries had high priests:

The Earthly High Priest	The Heavenly High Priest
For every **high priest** taken from among men is ordained for men in things pertaining to God, that he may offer both gifts and sacrifices for sins. Hebrews 5:1	But Christ being come an **high priest** of good things to come, by a greater and more perfect tabernacle, not made with hands, that is to say, not of this building. Hebrews 9:11

According to Scripture, both sanctuaries had sacrifices:

The Typical Sacrifice	The True Sacrifice
And every priest standeth daily ministering and offering oftentimes the same **sacrifices**, which can never take away sins. Hebrews 10:11	By the which will we are sanctified through the **offering** of the body of Jesus Christ once for all.. Hebrews 10:10

    Similar to the sacrifices that occurred in the Old Testament sanctuary, Jesus Christ was the sacrifice of the New Testament. And just like the sinner placed his hand on the head of the goat and transferred their sins to the innocent animal, Christ, who never sinned, allowed our sins to be placed upon Him:

Shadowy transfer of Sin	True transfer of sin
Wherefore have ye not eaten the sin offering in the holy place, seeing it is most holy, and God hath given it you to **bear**	So Christ was once offered to **bear the sins of many**; and unto them that look for him shall he appear the second time without sin

THE 2300-DAY PROPHECY • 45

the iniquity of the congregation, to make atonement for them before the LORD? Leviticus 10:17

unto salvation. Hebrews 9:28

Now I want you to contemplate this one thought: Most Christians believe that once Christ died on the cross, His work was finished; however, in the earthly sanctuary, the work was really just getting started. According to Scripture, the priest transferred the people's sins to the earthly sanctuary through the blood he carried into the Holy Place.[10] And it was in this same manner that Christ obtained eternal redemption for the world by transferring our sins to the True Sanctuary in heaven.

Blood of the Old Covenant
"But into the second went the high priest alone once every year, **not without blood**, which he offered for himself, and for the errors of the people." Hebrews 9:7

Blood of the New Covenant
"Neither by the blood of goats and calves, **but by his own blood** he entered in once into the holy place, having obtained eternal redemption for us." Hebrews 9:11

By now, I'm sure you are saying to yourself—Did he just say our sins were transferred to the Heavenly Sanctuary? That's exactly what I'm saying.

---

[10] In some cases the blood was not taken into the holy place; but the flesh was then to be eaten by the priest (see Leviticus 10:17).

I can understand that this concept may sound foreign...maybe even blasphemous. However, if Jesus, who is holy, can have our sins placed upon Him, then why is it beyond the pale for our sins to be transferred to the Heavenly Sanctuary? Is the Heavenly Sanctuary more holy than Christ Himself? Of course not! Just like the priest of the earthly sanctuary transferred the sins of the people to the typical sanctuary, Christ bore our sins and transferred them to the Heavenly Sanctuary.

Remember, Israel's sins were transferred to the sanctuary throughout the year resulting in a process to have those sins removed. The process to have those sins removed occurred on the Day of Atonement in the Most Holy Place.

If the earthly sanctuary had to be cleansed from the sins of the people, what do you think needed to happen in the Heavenly Sanctuary? Ladies and Gentlemen, the earthly was simply a model of the heavenly, and so, just as the earthly needed to be justified, the heavenly also needs to be justified:

> And almost all things are by the law purged with blood; and without shedding of blood is no remission. It was therefore necessary that the patterns of things in the heavens should be **PURIFIED** with these; **but the heavenly things themselves with better sacrifices than these.** Hebrews 9:22-23

Are you seeing this? The Bible says that the earthly sanctuary had to be purified with blood from earthly sacrifices, but the heavenly sanctuary has to be purified with better sacrifices!

If you aren't sure that the Bible is talking about the Day of Atonement, pay close attention to the language used a few verses earlier:

> Now when these things were thus ordained, the priests went always into the first tabernacle, accomplishing the service of God. But into the second went the high priest alone **once every year**, not without blood, which he offered for himself, and for the errors of the people. Hebrews 9:6-7

This once-every-year service refers to the Day of Atonement (see Leviticus 16:34). Just like the earthly sanctuary needed to be cleansed, the Heavenly Sanctuary also needed to be purified. However, this purification was not by the blood of animal sacrifices; the Heavenly Sanctuary could only accept the blood of Christ, who was the perfect sacrifice.

Now we are able to see what sanctuary began to be cleansed in the autumn of 1844. Daniel 8:14 made a stunning revelation, and we now understand that on October 22, 1844, Christ moved from the Holy Place to the Most Holy Place in the Heavenly Sanctuary.

The Bible foretold of this transition from one compartment of the Heavenly Sanctuary to the other compartment:

> Behold, I will send my messenger, and he shall prepare the way before me: and

the Lord, whom ye seek, **shall suddenly come to his temple**, even the messenger of the covenant, whom ye delight in: behold, he shall come, saith the LORD of hosts. Malachi 3:1

I saw in the night visions, and, behold, one like the Son of man came with the clouds of heaven, and **came to the Ancient of days**, and they brought him near before him. Daniel 7:13

What should we be doing while the heavenly sanctuary is being cleansed?

The Cleansing of the Sanctuary reveals to us that Jesus is in the final stages of His work as our High Priest. This doctrine also reveals to us that there is a work of judgment currently taking place in the Most Holy Place.

Remember, during the earthly Day of Atonement, the people were supposed to afflict their souls. Ladies and Gentlemen, we are supposed to be afflicting our souls as well:

The affliction of Israel	The Affliction of Christians
"And ye shall have on the tenth day of this seventh month an holy convocation; and **ye shall afflict your souls**..." Numbers 29:7	"**Be afflicted**, and mourn, and weep: let your laughter be turned to mourning, and your joy to heaviness." James 4:9

The Bible is not telling us that we should never laugh, or that we should always be in a state of depression; however, knowing the seriousness of the times, we should always remember to be soberminded, *looking unto Jesus the author and finisher of our faith* (Hebrews 12:2).

The Day of Atonement is a work of judgment
The Children of Israel understood that Yom Kippur was a time of judgment. Notice what happened to those who did not afflict their souls:

> "For whatsoever soul it be that shall not be afflicted in that same day, **he shall be cut off from among his people.**"
> Leviticus 23:29

There came a point in time that anyone who did not afflict their souls was cut off from God's people. The same is true today. There will come a time when anyone who is hasn't surrendered their heart to Christ will no longer have the opportunity to be saved. Their probation will be closed. Notice how John the Revelator conveys this idea:

> "**He that is unjust, let him be unjust still: and he which is filthy, let him be filthy still...**" Revelation 22:11

It is unfortunate, but not everyone will make it to heaven, and while the door of mercy is still open, we must understand that there is a cut-off period for that mercy. How do we know this? Because the Bible is clear that when Jesus comes, He will already have His reward with Him.

> "And, behold, I come quickly; and **my reward is with me,** to give every man according as his work shall be." Revelation 22:12

If Christ has His reward with Him, then this reveals that the saved and the lost will already have been determined when He comes through the clouds. If the saved and the lost are determined before the Second Coming, this reveals to us that there will be a judgment before Christ returns. According to John the Revelator, we are in that judgment time now:

> "And I saw another angel fly in the midst of heaven, having the everlasting gospel to preach unto them that dwell on the earth, and to every nation, and kindred, and tongue, and people, saying with a loud voice, Fear God, and give glory to him; for **the hour of his judgment is come...**" Revelation 14:6-7

Most Christians only focus on the White-throne Judgment; however, we must understand that this judgment occurs only to carry out the sentence of the heavenly judgment. If you are not clear on this point, think of it like this: Someone who is lost cannot decide to give his heart to Christ at the White-throne Judgment; their case has already been decided. We must understand that at the close of the heavenly Day of

Atonement, every individual will be stamped with either saved or lost.

Now do you see why the 2300-day prophecy is an important truth? It allows us to see that we are in the final phase of the sanctuary service, and that final phase includes one last act.

The Scapegoat

If you remember, the Day of Atonement featured one final act: According to Leviticus 16:21, the high priest of the earthly sanctuary placed the sins of the people onto the scapegoat and sent him away into the wilderness by the hand of a fit man.

Most Christians believe that Christ is the scapegoat. This is a logical conclusion. It is reasonable to believe that Christ would be the final bearer of our sins as the scriptures reiterate that Jesus bore our sins. However, while I do agree that Christ bore our sins, the evidence from scripture reveals that Christ cannot be the scapegoat. Here is my proof:

1. In the New Covenant, Jesus died for our sins. In the Old Covenant, the scapegoat was never sacrificed.
2. In the earthly sanctuary, there were two goats chosen. According to Leviticus 16:8, the High Priest *cast one lot for the LORD, and the other lot for the scapegoat.* Notice, only one goat was for the Lord, not both. If Christ was the scapegoat, both goats should have been for the Lord.
3. In the scheme of the earthly sanctuary, the scapegoat was sent away after the High Priest

transferred the sins to it from the sanctuary. If Christ is the scapegoat, then this would mean that all of our sins will, once again, be placed on Christ, and He will afterward be sent away into an uninhabited place, never to return.

From the evidence presented, I think it's safe to say that Christ cannot be the scapegoat. Well, if it's not Christ, then who is it? The answer is Satan.

You may be shocked to hear this, but not only will Satan bear the penalty for his sins, but he will also bear the penalty for the sins that he caused the redeemed to commit.

If you are still unsure about this final phase of the heavenly ministration, read the words of John the Revelator as he describes the heavenly fit man leading the real scapegoat into an uninhabited land:

> "And I saw an angel come down from heaven, having the key of the bottomless pit and a great chain in his hand. And he laid hold on the dragon, that old serpent, which is the Devil, and Satan, and bound him a thousand years, and cast him into the bottomless pit, and shut him up, and set a seal upon him, that he should deceive the nations no more, till the thousand years should be fulfilled: and after that he must be loosed a little season." Revelation 20:1-3

Do you see it? At the close of the earthly Day of Atonement, the sins of God's people were placed upon the scapegoat, and he was sent into an uninhabited land by the hand of a fit man. At the conclusion of the heavenly Day of Atonement, the confessed sins of God's people will be placed upon Satan, and he will be sent into a bottomless pit for a thousand years by the hand of an angel.

I'm sure someone reading this chapter may be wondering if I am suggesting that Satan ultimately dies for our sins. To prevent any confusion on this topic, let me make sure my position is clear: Jesus Christ is the One who died for our sins. He was treated as we deserve, that we might be treated as He deserves.[11] Once I am forgiven, it matters not whether my sins are placed at the bottom of the sea, on top of the moon, or onto the scapegoat. My salvation was secured through the perfect sacrifice of Christ. Satan is the instigator of sin. While I am responsible for my own actions, Satan must also be responsible for his.

If this is still unclear to you, let me give you a hypothetical scenario that can provide context: Imagine that you and an associate rob a bank. As the mastermind behind this heist, your associate convinces you to commit the actual crime while he waits outside in the getaway car. During the robbery, you get caught and arrested. On the day of your trial, you stand before the judge; however, because it's your first offense, the judge decides to make a deal with you. In exchange for your testimony against the mastermind, the judge will drop all charges against you. The mastermind, who has prior convictions and is known to be behind most crimes in the city, is arrested. The judge not only absolves you of

---

[11] Ellen White, Humble Hero p. 9

all wrongdoing, but he takes the sentence you would've received and places it on the mastermind as if he committed the crime all by himself!

Even though this is hypothetical, ask yourself this: Would you as the freed party be grateful to the judge or the mastermind? Even though the mastermind has to "bear" your sentence, did your freedom come from him or the judge who had mercy on you?

Ladies and Gentlemen, once we understand that Jesus was an innocent sacrifice, and Satan is the guilty scapegoat, we will then see that Satan isn't bearing our sins to save us. He is bearing our sins because he is the instigator of every sin that has, is, and will be committed. Once our sins are blotted out, we no longer are associated with that sin, and it's as if Satan committed the act all by himself. So even though Christ forgave us for our part in breaking his law, Satan must still pay for his part as the facilitator of all lawbreaking.

Hopefully, it's all becoming clear! The earthly sanctuary service not only revealed the sacrifice of our Savior, but it also revealed Satan's fate at the end of the world. The whole ministration of the earthly sanctuary revealed what was going to happen on a grand scale!

The Cleansing of the Sanctuary is important because it reveals what Jesus is doing right now. He is interceding for our sins, but he is also observing those of us who are afflicting our souls by having faith in His sacrifice and living by the power of His grace to put away sin. Praise God for our heavenly High Priest!

THE 2300-DAY PROPHECY • 55

Frequently Asked Questions about the 2300-day prophecy

Question: Where did Jesus go after His resurrection?
Answer: According to the Bible, Jesus left earth and sat next to His Father in His throne. Revelation 3:21 says, *"To him that overcometh will I grant to sit with me in my throne, even as I also overcame, and am **set down with my Father in his throne**."* Hebrews 10:12 says, *"But this man, after he had offered one sacrifice for sins for ever, sat down on the right hand of God."*

The Bible is clear, Jesus sat next to His Father in His Throne.

Question: What was Jesus doing before 1844?
Answer: Scriptures declares that upon His ascension, Jesus began interceding for us. Romans 8:34 says, *"It is Christ that died, yea rather, that is risen again, who is even at the right hand of God, **who also maketh intercession for us**."* The Scriptures also tell us, *"if any man sin, we have an advocate with the Father, Jesus Christ the righteous."* 1John 2:1.

Question: How do we know Jesus resided in the first compartment of the Heavenly Sanctuary?
Answer: In vision, John the Revelator saw Christ at the lampstand, which was in the first compartment of the earthly sanctuary.

> And **in the midst of the seven candlesticks** one like unto the Son of man, clothed with a garment down to

the foot, and girt about the paps with a
golden girdle. Revelation 1:13

If Christ was before the seven candlesticks, then this is an indication that Christ was ministering in the first compartment of the Heavenly Sanctuary.

Question: How could Christ dwell in the first compartment of the Sanctuary when He was next to His Father? Doesn't the Father permanently reside in the Most Holy Place?
Answer: In the model of the earthly sanctuary, there were times when God resided in the first compartment. Notice where God met with the Children of Israel:

> "This shall be a continual burnt offering throughout your generations at the door of the tabernacle of the congregation before the LORD: where I will meet you, to speak there unto thee." Exodus 29:42

The presence of God mainly resided in the Most Holy Place; however, we see that there were times when God would meet His people at the door of the tabernacle, which indicates His presence was also in the first compartment. From this text, it is likely that God the Father met Christ in the first compartment of the Heavenly Sanctuary, and that is where Jesus sat next to His Father, interceding for us.

Question: The Bible says that when Christ was resurrected, He went within the veil. Doesn't this mean

Jesus went into the Most Holy Place immediately after His resurrection?

Answer: The Bible is clear that Jesus did go within the veil after his resurrection.

> Which hope we have as an anchor of the soul, both sure and stedfast, and **which entereth into that within the veil**. Hebrews 6:19

However, what this scripture does not reveal is that there was more than one veil to the Sanctuary. There was a veil at the entrance of the Sanctuary often called the "*hanging for the door of the tent*,"[12] and there was a veil separating the Holy Place from the Most Holy Place. Notice how the veil that separated the Holy Place from the Most Holy Place was labeled:

> And after **the second veil**, the tabernacle which is called the Holiest of all; Hebrews 9:3

The Bible is clear. The *second* veil is what separated the Holy Place from the Most Holy Place; however, the scriptures never say that Jesus entered the second veil. This lines up with the evidence that suggests Christ initially entered the veil to the first compartment of the Heavenly Sanctuary.

Question: In the Old Testament, there were daily sacrifices, and then there was another sacrifice on the

---

[12] Exodus 26:36

Day of Atonement. How can both services point to Christ if Christ only died once?

Answer: It's impossible for the ministration of the earthly sanctuary service and the Heavenly Sanctuary service to be precisely the same. Let me show you why:
- In the earthly sanctuary service, the High Priest brought a goat to the sanctuary.
- In the heavenly sanctuary service, Christ was both the High Priest and the sacrifice.

- In the earthly sanctuary, the High Priest went into the sanctuary *with* the blood of the sacrifice.
- In the heavenly sanctuary service, Jesus entered the sanctuary *by* His own blood.

There are apparent differences between the earthly and the heavenly ministrations. However, these differences should be expected by the mere fact that the earthly sanctuary was ministered by mortal beings, and the Heavenly Sanctuary is ministered by a supernatural Being.

In the earthly sanctuary, there were daily sacrifices, and there was a yearly sacrifice on the Day of Atonement. If we expect the earthly ministration to be an exact replica of the Heavenly Sanctuary, then Christ would have to be crucified and resurrected every day. Then He would have to be crucified one more time, before the end of the world, for the heavenly Day of Atonement. Regarding this difference, the Bible is clear:

> Nor yet that he should offer himself often, as the high priest entereth into

the holy place every year with blood of others; For then must he often have suffered since the foundation of the world: but now once in the end of the world hath he appeared to put away sin by the sacrifice of himself. Hebrews 9:25-26

Christ's one-time sacrifice covered all the earthly sacrifices, including the Day of Atonement.

Question: I thought the blood of Jesus cleanses, how can His blood "pollute" the heavenly sanctuary?
Answer: The Scriptures never declared that Christ's blood polluted the sanctuary. However, if the earthly sanctuary was a model, then we must understand that Jesus' blood represents dual facets of the sanctuary service. In the earthly sanctuary service, one sacrifice allowed the sins to be transferred to the sanctuary, and another sacrifice allowed those sins to be removed from the sanctuary. If Christ's sacrifice was once for all, then Jesus' blood represents both facets.

Question: Before Jesus died on the cross, He said, *It is finished*. How can you say that there was more for Christ to do if He said His work was done?
Answer: John 19:30 does not mince words. It says, *"When Jesus therefore had received the vinegar, he said, It is finished: and he bowed his head, and gave up the ghost."*

Clearly, Christ fulfilled his perfect sacrifice at the cross; however, the Bible confirms that this finished work was not the completion of the heavenly ministration. How do we know this? Revelation 21:6

says, "And he said unto me, **It is done**. I am Alpha and Omega, the beginning and the end."

Yes, it was *finished* at the cross, but it's not *done* until Christ's work in the Heavenly Sanctuary is completed.

Question: How do we know the 2300 days were not accomplished by Antiochus Epiphanes?
Answer: You may not be aware of this, but much of the Evangelical world believes a king named Antiochus Epiphanes fulfilled the 2300-day prophecy. Even though Evangelicals are not unified on the start and end dates of this prophecy, most Evangelicals seem to believe the Syrian ruler's actions necessitated the cleansing of the earthly sanctuary.

Epiphanes did perform horrible acts against God's people; however, it should also be clear that he did not fulfill the 2300-day prophecy.

First, let's understand how some Evangelicals connect Antiochus Epiphanes to the 2300-day prophecy:

> "The interpretation of the period of time, 2300 evening-mornings, named by the angel is beset with difficulty. And first the verbal import of בקר ערב is doubtful. Among recent interpreters, Berth., Hv., v. Leng., Maur., and Horm. understand by its days consisting of morning and evening (twenty-four hours); others, as Bleek, Kirmss, Ewald, Hitzig, Wieseler, Kran., and Delitzsch,

are of opinion that evening-morning is particularly reckoned with reference to the offering of a morning and an evening sacrifice each day, so that 2300 evening-mornings make only 1150 whole days."[13]

In simplified terms, some Evangelicals believe the 2300 days are not days. When Daniel 8:14 says, "*Unto two thousand and three hundred days; then shall the sanctuary be cleansed,*" we must understand that the word "days" in the original language is translated from the Hebrew, *'ereḇ bōqer*, meaning evenings and mornings. The translators understood that *'ereḇ bōqer* is the same phrase that was used in Genesis when the Bible says, "... And the **evening** and the **morning** were the first day."[14] Instead of the translation declaring the sanctuary would be cleansed at the end of 2300 evenings and mornings, the translators simplified the phrase using everyday vernacular—hence the word *days*.

Some Evangelicals believe that this evening and morning phrase refers to the sacrifices of the earthly sanctuary. For example, Ezra 3:3 says,

"And they set the altar upon his bases; for fear was upon them because of the people of those countries: and they offered burnt offerings thereon unto the LORD, even burnt offerings **morning and evening.**

---

[13] Delitzsch, Franz, and Carl Friedrich Keil. 1857. Biblical commentary on the Old Testament. Edinburgh: T. & T. Clark.
[14] Genesis 1:5

2Chronicles 31:3 says,

> He appointed also the king's portion of his substance for the burnt offerings, to wit, for the **morning and evening** burnt offerings

1Chronicles 16:40 says,

> To offer burnt offerings unto the LORD upon the altar of the burnt offering continually **morning and evening**, and to do according to all that is written in the law of the LORD, which he commanded Israel;

The morning and evening sacrifices were essentially two sacrifices on the same day. Therefore, when Daniel 8:14 says, *Unto 2300 evenings and mornings*, some Evangelicals believe it was really 2300 evening and morning sacrifices—not days. If the scripture should be rendered, *Unto 2300 evening and morning sacrifices*, then that would equate to 1,150 days of dual sacrifices (2300 ÷ 2).

This *1150-day prophecy* is clever on the surface; however, accepting this as Biblical truth presents a number of problems:

> 1. If the original Hebrew says *evening and mornings*, but we decide it should be evening and morning sacrifices, we have just added to the Word of God, and Revelation 22:19 reveals how seriously God considers this offense.

2. If the events of the 2300 days referred to the period of desolation made by Antiochus Epiphanes, then when did these 2300 sacrifices occur? History reveals Antiochus Epiphanes desolated the sanctuary. If the sanctuary was desolated, how could there have been 1150 days of animal sacrifices?
3. When referring to the daily sacrifice, notice the Bible uses *mornings and evenings*. When Daniel speaks about the 2300 days, he says *evenings and mornings*. *Mornings and evenings* may relate to the daily sacrifice, but *evenings and mornings* relate to the first week of creation. Clearly, the 2300 evenings and the mornings refer to 2300 days, not sacrifices.
4. 3½ years after Antiochus desecrated the temple, it was reconsecrated on the 25th day of the 9th Hebrew month called Kislev (December 14).[15] Many Evangelicals believe this was the Cleansing of the Sanctuary declared by Daniel. However, we must remember God decreed that the Day of Atonement would only occur on the tenth day of the seventh month,[16] not the twenty-fifth day of the ninth month. If God deemed that the Day of Atonement would only fall on a specific day, then any

---

[15] Jews, Church & Civilization, Volume I. N.p.: David Birnbaum, (n.d.). p. 209
[16] Leviticus 16:29-34

attempt to "cleanse" the sanctuary on another day would be rejected by God.

Now that you have a better understanding of the 2300-day prophecy, I would like to end this chapter with a chart of this prophetic timeframe. We will build onto this chart as we progress in this book; however, here is what we have thus far:

Chapter 4

The 1260-Day Prophecy

> *And I heard the man clothed in linen, which was upon the waters of the river, when he held up his right hand and his left hand unto heaven, and sware by him that liveth for ever that it shall be for a time, times, and an half; and when he shall have accomplished to scatter the power of the holy people, all these things shall be finished."* Daniel 12:7

Out of all the time-based prophecies, the 1260 days are the most commonly referenced in Scripture. This prophecy was not only declared by Daniel but it was also revealed by John the Revelator.

Before we discover the meaning of this prophecy, I think it's in our best interest to document every verse that refers to the 1260-day timeframe. Documenting every instance of this prophecy will hopefully help us establish the context of its fulfillment. Let's carefully review these scriptures:

> And he shall speak great words against the most High, and shall wear out the saints of the most High, and think to change times and laws: and they shall

be given into his hand until **a time and times and the dividing of time.** Daniel 7:25

And I heard the man clothed in linen, which was upon the waters of the river, when he held up his right hand and his left hand unto heaven, and sware by him that liveth for ever that it shall be for **a time, times, and an half**; and when he shall have accomplished to scatter the power of the holy people, all these things shall be finished. Daniel 12:7

But the court which is without the temple leave out, and measure it not; for it is given unto the Gentiles: and the holy city shall they tread under foot **forty and two months.** Revelation 11:2

And I will give power unto my two witnesses, and they shall prophesy **a thousand two hundred and threescore days**, clothed in sackcloth. Revelation 11:3

And the woman fled into the wilderness, where she hath a place prepared of God, that they should feed her there **a thousand two hundred and threescore days.** Revelation 12:6

And to the woman were given two wings of a great eagle, that she might fly into the wilderness, into her place, where she is nourished for **a time, and times, and half a time**, from the face of the serpent. Revelation 12:14

And there was given unto him a mouth speaking great things and blasphemies; and power was given unto him to continue **forty and two months**. Revelation 13:5

Wow! The Bible refers to this 1260-day timeframe in seven different locations! I'm not sure if there's any significance to the number of times this prophecy is mentioned; however, we do know that the number seven has been frequently used by God. Either way, this book's focus is not about the frequency of this prophecy but rather the meaning behind it.

I believe the best way to understand the 1260-day prophecy is to understand the context of all seven verses. This context then becomes the criteria that our interpretation must meet. In essence, our interpretation of the 1260 days must match the picture painted by these seven verses. Let's build the criteria by first examining each scripture.

The saints will be given into his hand.
Daniel 7:25 says, *"And he shall speak great words against the most High, and shall wear out the saints of the most High, and think to change times and laws: and they shall be given into his hand until a time and times and the dividing of time."*

According to Daniel, there is a group of people

who will be given into someone's hand. In order to understand this verse, we need to determine who *they* are, who *he* is.

To understand who they are, we don't have to go far. The beginning of the scripture says *he shall wear out the saints of the most High.* It is clear that "they" are the saints of God. However, we don't know if *they* are saints of the Old Testament (i.e., Jews) or if *they* are saints of the New Testament (i.e., Christians). I believe the best approach in this situation is to determine who *he* is, and that will help us understand which phase of God's people is being described in verse 25.

"*He*" in verse 25 is the same entity that arose among the ten horns. Verse 24 says, "*And the ten horns out of this kingdom are ten kings that shall arise: and another shall rise after them; and he shall be diverse from the first, and he shall subdue three kings.*" It clear that the "*he*" in verses 24 and 25 is the Little Horn. For further information on the Little Horn, I suggest you read my book titled, *The Clear and Present Truth of the Abomination of Desolation.* In this book, I divulge that Daniel's vision in chapter 7 revealed the same four kingdoms that Nebuchadnezzar's dream introduced.

In Daniel 7, the prophet saw four beasts.

The first was like a lion.

A second, like to a bear.

A third like a leopard, which had upon the back of it four wings of a fowl.

Then the prophet saw a fourth beast. This one had ten horns.

We should understand that these four beasts of Daniel 7 represent the same four components of the image that Nebuchadnezzar saw in his dream.

A study of the Book of Daniel will reveal that these kingdoms were all world-ruling empires that encountered God's people during their time on the world's stage. In my book, *The Clear and Present Truth of the Seven Heads and Ten Horns*, I reveal that the clay mixed with the iron feet and toes represents the Papacy, a religious system that involved itself with the kingdoms of this world.

Rising to power after the fall of the Western Roman Empire, the Papacy was the religiopolitical entity that, according to Daniel, *wore out the saints of the Most High*.[17]

---

[17]Smith, Uriah. 1983. The prophecies of Daniel and the Revelation. Washington, D.C.: Review and Herald Pub. Association. pp. 111-112

Now that we understand *who they* are and who *he* is, we now can understand what really occurred during the 1260 years.

According to the Bible, the Little Horn gained supremacy over the saints of God sometime after the fall of the Western Roman Empire. History tells us that the Roman Empire fell in 476 AD,[18] which reveals the 1260 days began sometime after that year.

> **A Time, Times, and the Dividing of Time**
>
> According to Daniel 4:16, King Nebuchadnezzar was humbled for 7 times. Most Bible scholars agree this was a seven-year time span.
>
> So Biblically speaking a time equals one year.
>
> Remembering a prophetic year consisted of 360 days, the time, times, and dividing of times is calculated as follows:
>
> A time = 360 days
> Times = 720 days (360 + 360)
> Dividing of time = 180 days (360 ÷ 2)
> --------------------
> 1260 days
>
> In prophecy, it is often the case that a day equals a year. (see Numbers 14:34 and Ezekiel 4:6). Therefore, we conclude that this timeframe was 1260 years.

The power of the holy people will be scattered.

Daniel 12:7 says, "*...it shall be for a time, times, and an half; and when he shall have accomplished to scatter the power of the holy people, all these things shall be finished.*" This scripture reveals to us that during this 1260-day

---

[18] Wasson, Donald L. "Fall of the Western Roman Empire." World History Encyclopedia. Last modified April 12, 2018. https://www.worldhistory.org/article/835/fall-of-the-western-roman-empire/.

period, God's people would be scattered. The word scatter in the original language can also be defined as *broken or dashed to pieces*. This definition reveals that during the 1260 years, God's people would suffer persecution.

The Holy City will be trodden underfoot.

According to Revelation 11:2, "*the holy city shall they tread under foot forty and two months.*" In this verse, "*they*" represent the Gentiles, and the holy city refers to Jerusalem. However, we already established that this prophetic timeframe began sometime after 476 AD. If the trodding of the Holy City referred to literal Jerusalem, this prophecy should have begun in the first century, not the fifth century. History reveals the Romans destroyed Jerusalem in 70 AD. If the trampling of the Holy City referred to this destruction, then the 1260 years should have begun in 70 AD and ended in 1331 AD. Unfortunately, 1331 has never been considered the date that ended the trodding down of the Holy City, nor is the desolation of 70 AD considered the start of the trodding underfoot.

If we cannot determine a literal application of Revelation 11:2, we must consider a spiritual application. Revelation 11:1 says, "*And there was given me a reed like unto a rod: and the angel stood, saying, Rise, and measure the temple of God, and the altar, and them that worship therein.*" Some may believe the angel is referring to the earthly sanctuary in Jerusalem; however, that temple had been obliterated by the Romans almost 20 years earlier. It should therefore be understood that the temple of Revelation 11 refers to the

Heavenly Sanctuary! If you are not fully convinced, please read verse 19 of the same chapter, where John the Revelator saw this same temple of God, but it was *opened in heaven*. The temple of God in verse 1 is the same temple of God in verse 19. The question is, how can John measure the temple and them that worship there if he is on earth? This can be understood once we realize believers on earth are spiritually in heaven:

> "And hath raised us up together, and made us sit together in heavenly places in Christ Jesus." Ephesians 2:6

If believers are spiritually worshipping in the Heavenly Sanctuary, then believers must be spiritually located in the heavenly Jerusalem. Paul made it clear that the Jerusalem in heaven is where our focus should be when he declared, *"...Jerusalem which is above is free, which is the mother of us all."*[19]

If the Sanctuary and the Holy City represent heavenly places, then the outer court must represent the earth as verse 2 declares *it is given unto the Gentiles*. The Gentiles represent unbelievers; therefore, they are not in the heavenly places as are God's believers.

After detailing the Sanctuary and the Holy City, verse 2 declares that the Gentiles will tread the Holy City underfoot for forty and two months! How can the Holy City be trodden under foot if it's in heaven? Paul answers this question by making the following declaration to the Thessalonians:

---

[19] Galatians 4:26

> Who opposeth and exalteth himself above all that is called God, or that is worshipped; so that he as God sitteth in the temple of God, shewing himself that he is God. 2Thessalonians 2:4

Paul made a startling revelation. God's heavenly sanctuary would one day be under attack by the Antichrist. However, we must understand that this attack on the Heavenly Sanctuary doesn't mean the Antichrist literally travels into heavenly places. Understand that when a man requires you to confess your sins to him instead of God, he is interfering with Christ's heavenly ministration. This interference is how the Man of Sin spiritually sits in the Temple of God.

Similar to the attack made against God's Sanctuary, the Gentiles trodding down the Holy City is a literal attack upon God's people who are spiritually located in heavenly places. This trodding down of the Holy City represents Christian persecution. Daniel mentioned this same trodding upon God's people when he said,

> "The fourth beast shall be the fourth kingdom upon earth, which shall be diverse from all kingdoms, and shall devour the whole earth, and shall **tread it down**, and break it in pieces." Daniel 7:23

The 42-month timeframe represents the same period as 1260 years. Remembering a month in Bible prophecy represents 30 days, we simply multiply 30 by

42, and we will see this scripture is referring to the same timeframe: **30 x 42 = 1,260**

The Two Witnesses shall prophesy.
Revelation 11:3 reveals that God will give power to His two witnesses, "*and they shall prophesy a thousand two hundred and threescore days, clothed in sackcloth.*" This time-based prophecy refers to the same 1260 years; however, we must decipher who or what these two witnesses are.

The characteristics of the Two Witnesses are captured by John and are described as follows:
- The Witnesses prophesy for 1260 days clothed in sackcloth. (Revelation 11:3)
- When under attack, fire comes from the mouths of these Two Witnesses, or they will kill the attackers in the same manner that they are being attacked. (Revelation 11:5)
- The Witnesses have the power to prevent clouds from producing rain. (Revelation 11:6)
- The Witnesses have control over water and can turn it into blood. (Revelation 11:6)
- The Witnesses have the ability to smite the earth with all plagues as often as they desire. (Revelation 11:6)
- At the end of the 1260 years, a beast shall make war against them and kill them. (Revelation11:7)
- The Witnesses' dead bodies will lie unburied in the streets of a great city called Sodom and Egypt, resulting in the world rejoicing. (Revelation 11:8-10)

- All of a sudden, the Two Witnesses come back to life, which terrifies the world. The Witnesses then ascend to heaven in a cloud. (Revelation 11:11-12)

Wow! This sounds like a blockbuster movie of epic proportions! As I read the description given by John, I envisioned two men appearing out of nowhere. They are wearing hooded medieval garments that obscure their faces while walking the streets of a crowded Middle Eastern city. Everyone who looks at them feels some inexplicable power attached to these men. (Don't fast forward, the movie is about to get better!) Suddenly, the men take off their hoods and begin to prophesy in the streets of that city! People from all over the Muslim world come to hear the Witnesses speak about Jesus and His Second Coming.

Then out of nowhere, some zealous Islamic militants try to attack the Witnesses, but the Witnesses open their mouths, and fire shoots out, burning the flesh off the evil men's bones (And there goes our G-rating out the window)!

Every time someone tries to kill these Witnesses, it fails. If someone shoots at the Witnesses, those bullets come back towards the attackers. If they fire a grenade launcher, that missile comes back around like a heat-seeking boomerang! The power that these Witnesses wield is unmatched by anything we've ever seen! They control water like the Greek god Poseidon! They control rain, and if they desire, the water turns into blood. These are very powerful individuals!

As soon as they've finished preaching, a gigantic sea monster bursts through the ocean floor and ascends into the open sky. It has red eyes with wings so long they block the sun. The creature has supernatural hearing. Its ears detect the two voices it has been summoned to destroy. Like a vulture smelling its roadkill, the beast locates the Two Witnesses preaching in the center of this great city. The monster lands on the street, which sends the crowds scattering like cats in the thunderstorm.

The Two Witnesses see the monster, but they are not scared because they know they are all-powerful. They lift their hands and send plagues towards the beast, but to their surprise, the beast is not fazed. Plague after plague hits the beast, but the beast doesn't seem to be bothered by these combos!

The beast then opens his mouth, and a blue ray of fire comes out and strikes both witnesses. They stagger, shocked that they've met their match. The sea monster then sends the final blow. His eyes and mouth light up with the same blue light, and this time the beam hits them so hard it creates a mushroom cloud of blue smoke.

After several minutes of silence, the smoke clears, revealing an enormous crater where the blast struck. In the center of that crater are the dead bodies of the Two Witnesses. News stations are there to report this. People are going live on social media to share this. Once everyone sees that these Witnesses are dead, waves of cheering and rejoicing are heard around the world! The Witnesses are dead!

This cheering continues for about three and half days until someone captures live video footage of the Two Witnesses alive! There they are, standing in the streets again! But this time, a voice is heard, and a cloud takes them to heaven in the presence of all the bad people—the end.

There's a lot of mystery surrounding these two witnesses. Are they Elijah and Moses? Are they angels from heaven? An important point to remember is that the Book of Revelation contains a lot of symbolism. Therefore, if texts within Revelation cannot be taken literally, then consider a symbolic interpretation. If we are to consider the Two Witnesses literal, we would have to believe that:

1. God, who instructs believers to turn the other cheek,[20] plans to send two individuals who will retaliate against anyone who provokes them.
2. All the beasts of Revelation are literal. This means all the beasts that John saw were real living creatures.
3. God will pull two people out of the heavenly paradise and send them back to earth just to preach and be killed. Jesus already died for the world...why would the Witnesses need to do the same?

These three points contain enough evidence that would cause me to question the literalness of this story. While many believers take a literal approach to the Two Witnesses, I honestly believe we have enough information to decipher the symbols and pinpoint what event is being described.

---

[20] Matthew 5:39

Notice John the Revelator called the Two Witnesses *the two olive trees, and the two candlesticks standing before the God of the earth.* This language appears to be strikingly similar to something the Prophet Zechariah uttered long before John:

> And **two olive trees** by it, one upon the right side of the bowl, and the other upon the left side thereof. So I answered and spake to the angel that talked with me, saying, What are these, my lord?... Then he answered and spake unto me, saying, **This is the word of the LORD** unto Zerubbabel, saying, Not by might, nor by power, but by my spirit, saith the LORD of hosts. Zechariah 4:3-4,6

A few verses later, the prophet asked the same question:

> "Then answered I, and said unto him, What are these **two olive trees** upon the right side of the **candlestick** and upon the left side thereof? And I answered again, and said unto him, What be these two olive branches which through the two golden pipes empty the golden oil out of themselves? And he answered me and said, Knowest thou not what these be? And I said, No, my lord. Then said he, **These are the two anointed ones, that stand by the Lord of the whole earth.**" Zechariah 4:11-14

It should be clear that the Two Anointed Ones weren't literal people. Represented by the two olive trees, the angel previously said they represented the Word of the Lord to Zerubbabel. In essence, the Two Anointed Ones represented God's Word. The fact that there were two Anointed Ones may indicate that one of the Anointed may be the Old Testament, and the other Anointed could be the New Testament.

With this understanding, we can now make sense of the attack on the Two Witnesses in Revelation. Considering the Witnesses represent the Bible (the combination of the Old and New Testaments), we now see that sometime after 476 AD, there was an attack on God's Word. Regarding this attack on the Bible, history documents various decrees that refer to this attack. One such law was called the Decree of the Council of Toulouse:

> "We prohibit also that the laity should be permitted to have the books of the Old or New Testament; but we most strictly forbid their having any translation of these books." *Decree of the Council of Toulouse* (1229 C.E.)

The attack on the Two Witnesses was rooted in the fact that the Papacy forbade people to have the Word of God. This prohibition is why the Two Witnesses were clothed in sackcloth.

It should also be evident why the Witnesses had the power to control the rain and turn water into blood. When God instructed individuals to perform miracles, it was through God's Word that these miracles were performed. There is power in the Word of God! Regarding the plagues, the Bible says,

> "For I testify unto every man that heareth the words of the prophecy of this book, If any man shall add unto these things, God shall add unto him the plagues that are written in this book." Revelation 22:18

Regarding those who are killed in the same manner that they attacked the Two Witnesses, the Bible says,

> "And if any man shall take away from the words of the book of this prophecy, God shall take away his part out of the book of life, and out of the holy city, and from the things which are written in this book." Revelation 22:19

Ladies and Gentlemen, we are looking for a 1260-year period in which the Word of God was attacked. It appears that having a Bible was illegal, and so the sackcloth represented obscurity. However, there's also a three-and half-year period in which an attempt to eradicate the Bible was made. This attempt appears to have failed, and the Word of God afterward spread like wildfire.

The woman fled into the wilderness.

Revelation 12:6 reveals a *woman who fled into the wilderness for a thousand two hundred and threescore days.* Verse 14 of the same chapter shows that God gave this woman *wings of a great eagle,* and she was able to *fly into the wilderness* for a *time, times, and a half of time.*

We should understand that this woman is symbolic. We know women don't have wings (even though my wife often threatens to fly away), and we know that no creature can create a flood with its saliva (see verse 16).

The woman of Revelation 12 represents God's people in both phases. God said to the Children of Israel, *"Turn, O backsliding children, saith the LORD; for I am married unto you."*[21] Paul said to the Christian believers, *"For I am jealous over you with godly jealousy: for I have espoused you to one husband, that I may present you as a chaste virgin to Christ."*[22] The woman in Revelation 12 represents the Israelites of the Old Covenant but also represents the Christian Church of the New Covenant.

Revelation 12:5 brings our attention to the Crucifixion of Christ; then verses 6 and 14 focuses on the 1260 years. The fact that the 1260 years is mentioned after the Crucifixion indicates the woman under attack in verses 6 and 14 represents the New Covenant phase of God's people called the Christian Church. The chapter makes it evident that at some point after Christ's Resurrection, the New Testament Church would find itself under attack by the Dragon.

Power was given to the Beast.

According to Revelation 13:5, a beast was given power to continue 42 months (1260 years). Now let's see if we can determine the identity of this Beast.

---

[21] Jeremiah 3:14
[22] 2Corinthians 11:2

John the Revelator begins this chapter by declaring he saw a Beast with seven heads and ten horns. This description is strikingly similar to the Beast that Daniel saw, which also had ten horns![23]

Students of prophecy should understand that Daniel's ten-horned Beast was none other than the Roman Empire. If you recall, Daniel saw four beasts, and we determined that the fourth Beast was the Roman Empire. Daniel then revealed that a Little Horn would rise among Rome's ten horns. The description that Daniel gave to the Little Horn matches the description John gave to the Beast of Revelation 13:

- Daniel 7:8 says the Little Horn had "*a mouth speaking great things.*"
- Revelation 13:5 says the Beast had "*a mouth speaking great things.*"

- Daniel 7:21 says the "*horn made war with the saints.*"
- Revelation 13:7 says, "*it was given unto him to make war with the saints.*"

- Daniel 7:25 says the saints "*shall be given into his hand until a time and times and the dividing of time.*"
- Revelation 13:5 says, "*power was given unto him to continue forty and two months.*"

Clearly, the Little Horn who rose out of Rome and the Beast of Revelation 13:1 refer to the same power. In

---

[23] Daniel 7:7

order to understand who these entities are, we must understand history. After 476 AD, the Western Roman Empire broke up into a number of smaller kingdoms. However, after the breakup in the west, the Bishop of Rome obtained Emperor-like powers, and he began to rule Church and State in the west. We will explore the rise of the Papacy, but first, let's combine all the clues we've learned about the 1260-year period:

Evidence for the 1260-year prophecy

Now that we've analyzed every scripture that refers to the 1260-year timeframe, we now have enough information to determine what occurred during this period and establish when this period began and ended.

According to the Bible, for 1260 years...

- Power would be given to the Papacy.
- The Word of God would be under attack.
- The saints would be given into the Papacy's hand
- The Church would be scattered.
- The Church would be trodden underfoot.
- The Church would go into hiding.

Now that we've documented all the events that occurred during the 1260 years, we can clearly see the picture that the Bible paints for us.

The Bible reveals that at some point after the breakup of the Roman Empire, the Papacy would be given Emperor-like powers. Using its authority over

Church and State, the Papacy would begin to suppress the Word of God. The suppression of Scripture would place Bible-believing Christians at the mercy of the Papacy, and they would be given into his hand via persecution. This persecution would result in the scattering of true Bible believers and ultimately force the Church into hiding for 1260 years. Towards the end of this period, a nation would make war against the Bible for 3 ½ years. Many historians believe it was the nation of France that embraced atheistic views from November 1793 to June 1797.[24]

Now that we know what happened, we can direct our focus on when it occurred. We must determine what year the Papacy came into this power, and then we must see a decline in that power 1260 years later.

History reveals that the dates for this supremacy began in 538 AD.

"They invaded Italy, and conquered the Heruli in 493; and were defeated in 538 by Justinian, when the Pope was placed in quiet possession of the capital of Rome." *Sylvester Bliss, A Brief Commentary on the Apocalypse, p. 169*

---

[24] Waller, J. C.. The Second Coming of Christ: The Restitution of All Things, and Our Lord's Personal Reign with His Glorified Saints in His Millennial Kingdom on the Earth. United States: Waller, Sherrill & Company, 1865, p. 287

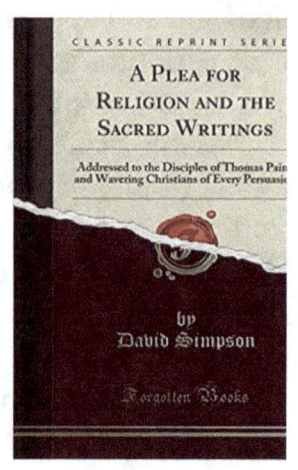

"Is it not extremely remarkable, and a powerful confirmation of the truth of Scripture prophecy, that just 1260 years ago from the present **1,798**, in the very beginning of the year **538**, Belisarius put an end to the empire of the Goths at Rome, leaving no power therein but the Bishop of that Metropolis?" *David Simpson, A Plea for Religion and the Sacred Writings, p. 166*

"Down to the sixth century all popes are declared saints in the martyrologies. Vigillius (**537-555**) is the first of a series of popes who no longer bear this title, which is henceforth sparingly conferred. From this time on the popes, more and more enveloped in worldly events, no longer belong solely to the church; they are men of the state, and then rulers of the state." *Belmont and Monod Medieval Europe, p. 120*

MEDIEVAL EUROPE FROM 395 TO 1270

"[The Roman Emperor] Justinian...enriched himself with the property of all 'heretics' - that is, non-Catholics; published edicts in **538 AD** compelling all to join the Catholic church in 90 days or leave the empire and confiscated all their goods."
Dr. N Summerbell, History of the Christian Church pp. 310-311

According to the historical records, the Papacy came into supreme power in the year 538 AD. Counting 1260 years forward brings us to the year 1798 AD. If our prophetic lens is properly focused, we should see evidence of Papal decline in that year.

Regarding 1798 AD, the encyclopedia states the following:

> "General Berthier marched to Rome, entered it unopposed on 10 February **1798**, and, proclaiming a Roman Republic, demanded of the pope the renunciation of his temporal authority."
> *Encyclopædia Britannica (11th ed.)*

History records that the Pope was taken captive by the French General, Louis-Alexandre Berthier. Eventually, another Pope was elected to power, but the Papacy never held the same authority from that time to the present.

While many of my Evangelical brethren believe the 1260-day prophecy is a future event, I believe the Bible gives us ample evidence to show that the 1260 years occurred during the Dark Ages of Papal supremacy.

Now that we've established the dates for the 1260-day prophecy, we can add this prophetic timeframe to our chart on the next page.

Chapter 5

The Answer to "How Long"

If you recall, Daniel 8 revealed a conversation between two angels. According to Daniel, one angel asked another angel, "*How long shall be the vision concerning the daily sacrifice, and the transgression of desolation, to give both the sanctuary and the host to be trodden under foot?*" You should also remember it is my assertion that the angel never answered this specific question; instead, he looked at Daniel and said, "*Unto two thousand and three hundred days; then shall the sanctuary be cleansed.*"

In case you are unaware, the Cleansing of the Sanctuary is an entirely different subject than the Daily Sacrifice, the Transgression of Desolation, and the trodding upon the host. If so, how could the angel answer the question with a prophetic event that was completely unrelated? Simple. The angel's answer revealed that by the time the Cleansing of the Sanctuary would begin in 1844, the Daily Sacrifice, the Transgression of Desolation, and the trodding upon the sanctuary and host would have already been fulfilled. If you are unclear on this point, let me give you an example to help you understand: One day, my wife called me on the phone and informed me that she was still at work and would most likely arrive home an hour late. I asked her if there was anything she needed me to do, to which she responded by asking if I could clean the kitchen and take out the trash. However, being the good husband that I am, I ended up cleaning the whole house! Later, I called to check on her to find out if she had left work. She informed me that she was leaving and asked me if I had cleaned the kitchen and taken out the trash. Instead of responding specifically about the trash and the kitchen, I simply informed her that I had cleaned the whole house. Understand, even though I did not answer her specific question, she understood that cleaning the whole house included the kitchen and the trash. So even though I didn't answer her specific question, my answer still satisfied her inquiry.

Similar to this example, the angel, while not answering the specific question, still satisfied the inquiry because the vision of the Daily Sacrifice, the Transgression of Desolation, and the trodding upon the sanctuary and host would all be fulfilled by the time the Cleansing of the Sanctuary was to commence. However, if we believe these events were fulfilled sometime *after* the Cleansing of the Sanctuary, then the answer given by the angel would've been completely unrelated to the question, potentially causing confusion regarding those prophecies. Since we know God is not the author of confusion, it is evident that the answer to "How long," was before Cleansing of the Sanctuary began in 1844 AD.

Knowing the vision of the Daily Sacrifice, the Transgression of Desolation, and the trodding of the host was fulfilled before 1844 is good, but it still doesn't tell us exactly when these prophecies were fulfilled.

Is it possible the angel asked a specific question, and God decided to leave us in suspense? I think not. What I need you to understand is that the answer to "*How long*" was actually answered...just not in chapter 8. However, before we find the answer to the "How long" question, we first must notice a few things revealed in Daniel 8.

First, let's observe the scene of Daniel's vision:

> "And I saw in a vision; and it came to pass, when I saw, that I was at Shushan in the palace, which is in the province of Elam; and I saw in a vision, and **I was by the river of Ulai**." Daniel 8:2

It important that you notice Daniel was by a river. You may not realize it at this moment, but this river is the key to understanding the answer to "*How long*."

Next, notice what Daniel heard and where the voice came from:

> "And I heard a man's voice **between the banks of Ulai**, which called, and said, Gabriel, make this man to understand the vision." Daniel 8:16

Notice, Daniel heard a Man's voice *between* the banks of the river. It is essential to understand that this voice didn't come from the banks or the sides of the river. The fact that the voice came from between the banks means the Individual who spoke was hovering over the middle of the water.

Now, if we go to Daniel 12, notice the scene of this vision:

> "Then I Daniel looked, and, behold, there stood other two, the **one on this side of the bank of the river, and the other on that side of the bank of the river.**" Daniel 12:5

Wow! Do you notice any similarities between Daniel's vision in chapter 8 and his vision in chapter 12? Though chapter 12 doesn't provide the river's name, the parallels between both visions should catch your attention. Notice two angels are standing on both sides of the river, and again, one of the angels asks a question:

> "And one said to the man clothed in linen, which was upon the waters of the river, How long shall it be to the end of these wonders?" Daniel 12:6

Are you seeing this? The angel from Daniel 8 asked, "**How long** *shall be the vision concerning the daily sacrifice, and the transgression of desolation, to give both the sanctuary and the host to be trodden under foot?*" And here in Daniel 12, the angel asks, "**How long** *shall it be to the end of these wonders?*"

Both visions feature a river, and both visions call our attention to an angel asking, "*how long.*" Coincidence? Not a chance! Once we see the similarities, it will become clear that the conversation in Daniel 8 is connected to the conversation in Daniel 12. However, this time, someone else answers the question that was asked. Notice who answers the question and where this Individual was located:

> "And I heard the man clothed in linen, which was **upon the waters of the river**, when he held up his right hand and his left hand unto heaven, and sware by him that liveth for ever that it shall be for a time, times, and an half; and when he shall have accomplished to scatter the power of the holy people, all these things shall be finished." Daniel 12:7

Notice the Man clothed in linen wasn't on the banks of the river—He was *upon* the river. Ladies and Gentlemen, do you remember the location of the voice Daniel heard in chapter 8? Daniel said, "*And I heard a man's voice between the banks of Ulai.*" It is clear to me that the voice Daniel *heard* between the banks of the river in chapter 8 was the same Individual he *saw* upon the waters of the river in chapter 12! The voice Daniel heard, and the Man clothed in linen was non-other than our Lord and Savior Jesus Christ!

Now it's becoming clear, Jesus showed up to give Daniel the specific answer to the specific question asked in Daniel 8. Jesus didn't mince words; He lifted His hands and told Daniel, "*it shall be for a time, times, and an half; and when he shall have accomplished to scatter the power of the holy people, all these things shall be finished.*"

In the fourth chapter of this book, we learned that the *time, times,* and *an half* represents the 1260 years of persecution. If you remember, Daniel was shown what the Little Horn would do to God's people.

According to Daniel 8:10-12, the Papal power would do the following:

1. Wax great, even to the host of heaven.

2. Cast down some of the host and of the stars to the ground, and stamp upon them.

3. Magnify himself even to the prince of the host.

4. Take away the Daily Sacrifice and cast down the place of his sanctuary.

5. Cast the truth down to the ground by reason of transgression.

Here, Jesus let the prophet know that all the horrible things he saw the Little Horn do would end at the conclusion of the 1260-year prophecy in 1798.

But Jesus didn't stop there. He then made this remarkable declaration to the prophet:

"And from the time that the daily sacrifice shall be taken away, and the abomination that maketh desolate set up, there shall be **a thousand two hundred and ninety days**. Blessed is he that waiteth, and cometh to **the thousand three hundred and five and thirty days**." Daniel 12:11-12

Later in this book, you will see that the 1290-day prophecy and the 1335-day prophecy were the result of the conversation in Daniel 8. However, the question we now must answer is—What are the 1290-day and the 1335-day prophecies?

Chapter 6

The 1290-Day Prophecy

> *And from the time that the daily sacrifice shall be taken away, and the abomination that maketh desolate set up, there shall be a thousand two hundred and ninety days.* Daniel 12:11

After Jesus reiterated how long the Papal persecution would last, he then introduced a new timeframe to Daniel. Some students of prophecy may be confused by this new timespan that almost seems to come out of leftfield. However, knowing Daniel 12 is connected to Daniel 8 helps us understand that Jesus is answering a question that was originally asked in chapter 8. In case you forgot this question, let me remind you:

> Then I heard one saint speaking, and another saint said unto that certain saint which spake, How long shall be the vision concerning the daily sacrifice, and the transgression of desolation, to give both the sanctuary and the host to be trodden under foot? Daniel 8:13

We understand that the 2300-day prophecy was fulfilled by 1844. We also understand that the Papal persecution of God's people was finished by 1798. However, the question in Daniel 8:13 was strictly related to the Daily Sacrifice and the Abomination of Desolation.[25]

You may be unaware, but the 1290-prophecy specifically addressed the length of time that would pass before the Daily Sacrifice would be replaced by the Abomination of Desolation. If you are unclear of the meaning of the Daily Sacrifice and the Abomination of Desolation, I suggest you read my books titled, *The Clear and Present Truth of the Daily Sacrifice* and *The Clear and Present Truth of the Abomination of Desolation*. In these books, I provide detailed information regarding these two prophetic events, which, I believe, serves as a pretext to understanding the 1290 days.

Before we break down the true meaning of the 1290-day prophecy, let's review how some individuals explain this mysterious timeframe.

508 AD?

A number of Bible scholars believe 508 AD is the starting point for the 1290-day prophecy. In the past, I have supported this position; however, I have since abandoned this viewpoint as I believe God has given us more information. Before we discuss this additional information, let's explore why many believe 508 was the starting point for the 1290-day prophecy. Here's how one author explains this position:

---

[25] The Transgression of Desolation is also called the Abomination of Desolation.

"Thus, there is indisputable historical confirmation and legislative documentation that 'the one and true Catholic faith' was indeed 'set up' or established as prophesied. With 'Catholic Law' 'commanded' to be 'preserved unimpaired,' and with the exclusivity of the bishops' jurisdiction in ecclesiastical affairs legally fixed. Clovis had become the first Catholic king of the ten symbolic horns of the Western Roman Empire dating from A.D. 476. **His ascension to the throne in 508** brought in its train the first instituted 'National' religion. All other faiths were outlawed. Then began the long chain reaction in prophetic history until every European nation accepted the one and true Catholic faith and was led to follow the example of the Franks in using the civil power to enforce the church's dogmas!" *Heidi Heiks, AD 508 Source Book, p 60*

One of my favorite authors stated it like this:

"**Thus in A.D. 508 terminated united resistance to the development of the papacy.** The question of supremacy between Frank and Goth, between the Catholic and the Arian religions, had then been settled in favor of the Catholics." *Uriah Smith, Daniel and Revelation, p 331*

From what I gather, these two quotes are trying to make the case that 508 was the year Roman Catholic supremacy really began. It seems that these scholars were looking at the supremacy of the Catholic Church like an avalanche. The avalanche hit in 538 AD, but a little ball of snow began rolling in 508 AD. In essence, the supremacy that the Papacy gained in 508 was like a forerunner to the supremacy it utilized in 538. If we calculate this timeframe beginning with 508, we will soon realize that 1290 years later takes us to 1798 AD. In essence, these authors are saying the 1260 years are *cut out* of the 1290 years.

I do understand why many view 508 as the starting point for the 1290-day prophecy. On the surface, it makes perfect sense. 508 can be seen as the first level of supremacy, and 538 can be seen as the second level of supremacy. Even though I can see the logic in this perspective, studying the Book of Daniel for myself made me realize 508 cannot be the starting point for the 1290-day prophecy. Please don't misunderstand my words. I'm not suggesting that 508 lacks any spiritual significance, I just realized that that year had little bearing on the Daily Sacrifice being replaced by the Abomination of Desolation.

For most of my adult life, I believed that the Daily Sacrifice being taken away and the Abomination of Desolation being set up represented Catholicism replacing Paganism. However, we are starting to see that Paganism was not the Daily Sacrifice, nor was the overtaking of Paganism by Catholicism the Abomination of Desolation.

For those of you who are unable to obtain copies of the two books I mentioned earlier, please allow me to define the Daily Sacrifice and the Abomination of Desolation:

The Daily Sacrifice

The Daily Sacrifice is not a sacrifice. As mentioned in Daniel 8:11-13, 11:31, and 12:11, "*Sacrifice*," which is attached to "*the Daily*," is not part of the original text. The King James translators often added words to this English translation to ensure the scriptures grammatically flowed. The King James Bible identifies these added words by italicizing them. Unfortunately, the translators erroneously added the word "*Sacrifice*" to the Daily. This erroneous addition is the source of much confusion. Some believe the Daily Sacrifice points to Antiochus Epiphanes, and others believe it points to the downfall of Paganism in the Roman Empire. Unfortunately, both are wrong.

The Daily in the original language means "*Continual*." The reason the translators added Sacrifice to this word is that Continual is often associated with the sanctuary service. The translators had difficulty understanding how the Continual could be taken away without it being related to the sanctuary.

The Continual is not a continual sacrifice. The Continual is the Continuation of the Jewish nation under the name of the Christian Church. The Church has not replaced Israel; the Church is the CONTINUATION of Israel. This is why Paul said, "*There is neither Jew nor*

Greek, there is neither bond nor free, there is neither male nor female: for ye are all one in Christ Jesus. And if ye be Christ's, then are ye Abraham's seed, and heirs according to the promise."[26] This is why God's messenger to the Gentiles also said, *"For he is not a Jew, which is one outwardly; neither is that circumcision, which is outward in the flesh: But he is a Jew, which is one inwardly; and circumcision is that of the heart, in the spirit, and not in the letter; whose praise is not of men, but of God."*[27]

Once you understand that the New Testament Church is the CONTINUATION of Israel, then you can understand that the taking away of the Continual was the taking away of true Christianity in the Roman Empire. As a matter of fact, every time Daniel mentioned the Daily being taken away, you will discover that chapter also mentions God's people being persecuted. True Christianity was persecuted; thus, it was in this manner that the *Daily* was taken away.

The Abomination of Desolation

The Abomination of Desolation relates to the Roman Catholic Church. However, the Abomination of Desolation does not involve Paganism relinquishing its dominion over the Roman Empire. It is true that Paganism was eventually overtaken by Catholicism, but that doesn't represent the Abomination of Desolation. The Abomination of Desolation was referred to by Christ when He said, *"When ye therefore shall see the abomination of desolation, spoken of by Daniel the prophet,*

---

[26] Galatians 3:28-29
[27] Romans 2:28-29

stand in the holy place, (whoso readeth, let him understand:)."[28]

If we recognize the event Jesus was referring to, then we should know that He was pointing towards the destruction of Jerusalem in 70 AD. Luke 21:20 revealed that the Abomination was when the Disciples would see *Jerusalem compassed with* [the Roman] *armies*. You must understand that when this Pagan army brought all their Pagan banners and surrounded the Holy City, this was an Abomination. This Abomination would later result in the destruction or Desolation of Jerusalem.

Once we understand how Christ defined the Abomination of Desolation, we can then understand that this definition never changes. The Abomination of Desolation is when Paganism invades God's territory. To simplify this statement, we can say, the Abomination of Desolation occurs when the religion of the occult or its practices are mixed with the religion of Jehovah.

In 70 AD, Pagan soldiers surrounded the grounds of the Holy City, creating an Abomination that resulted in Desolation. However, Daniel pointed to a second Abomination of Desolation. This second Abomination of Desolation occurred when Paganism merged with Christianity in 538 AD.

To say the Abomination of Desolation is Roman Catholicism is true, but in some respects, it's a misnomer. The Abomination of Desolation is not a person, place, or thing; it's an action. If this is unclear, let me give you an example: Google is an internet search engine, which means Google is a noun. However, I've

---

[28] Matthew 24:15

heard people say, "*I am going to Google it.*" In this manner, they are using Google as an action word, even though Google is technically a noun.

If you can understand that example, then you can understand that the Abomination of Desolation is a verb; it's an action. It's when the Holy is amalgamated with the profane. It's when good is merged with evil. Understand, when we call the Catholic Church the Abomination of Desolation, we are using that phrase as a noun. Using the Abomination of Desolation as a noun is acceptable, but please be aware that in its purest sense, the Abomination of Desolation is the act of merging good with evil. Because Roman Catholicism embraced and embodies this blending, it is appropriate to describe the Roman Catholic System as the Abomination of Desolation.

Now that we understand what the Daily and the Abomination of Desolation are, we can now understand that the transition from the Daily to the Abomination of Desolation occurred in 538 AD. Once Emperor Justinian declared the Bishop of Rome the supreme leader over the Christian Church, this was the turning point for God's people. The true Church was taken away, and a hybrid of Christianity and Paganism was set up.

The taking away of the Daily was so thorough that even to this day, many Christians and non-Christians believe Catholicism was the original Church established by Christ. I've conversed with Catholics on a variety of Biblical doctrines, and all of them conveyed the same sentiment—the sentiment that says the Catholic Church existed thousands of years before any other Christian denomination; therefore, all other churches, denominations, and belief systems are false. While I vehemently disagree with this position, I also understand why they believe in the authenticity of the Catholic Church. Catholics believe their church was the original because prophecy declared the Daily would be taken away and replaced by the Abomination of Desolation.

But I digress. Ladies and Gentlemen, are you starting to see why the transition from the Daily to the Abomination of Desolation has little to do with 508? Furthermore, if the taking away of Paganism is the focus for the 1290 days, the prophecy should not be parallel to the 1260 days. Let me explain:

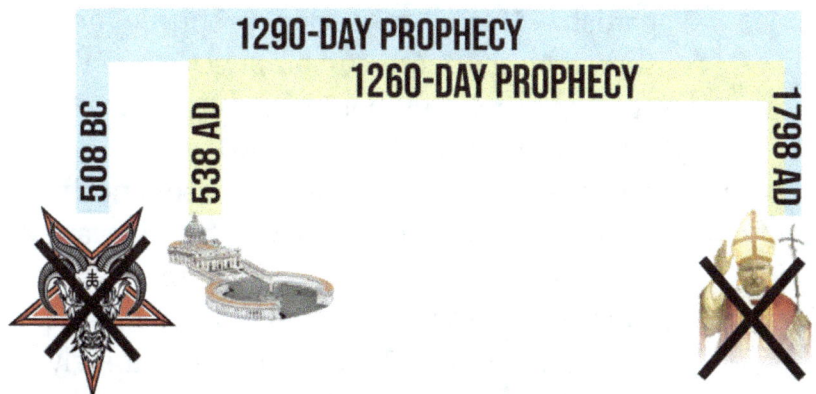

As shown above, proponents of the 508 starting point believe the 1290-day prophecy began in 508 with the decline of Paganism and the rise of Catholicism. For the next 30 years, the Papacy would be the supreme religion over Paganism. However, in 538, the Papacy's territory would increase with additional authority over Christianity.

In theory, this sounds good, but the more I pondered this position, the more I realized that it presents a few problems.

1. If the 1290-prophecy represented Papal supremacy over Paganism, and that supremacy ended in 1798 AD, shouldn't we have seen a revival of Paganism after 1798 AD? The previously sealed prophecies of Daniel were unsealed after 1798, and truth began to blossom; however, I've yet to see anyone suggest that Paganism also flourished after 1798 AD. If the 1290-day prophecy is about Paganism, then it must remain about Paganism. If the 1290-day prophecy gets absorbed by the 1260-day prophecy, then the 1290-day prophecy should be relegated to a 30-day prophecy (508 AD-538 AD).
2. The taking away of Paganism is prophetically relevant, but I don't believe it's relevant enough for God to assign a time-based prophecy towards its fulfillment. You must understand that Catholicism is merely Paganism with a Christian mask. Many Catholic Christians love the Lord and are good people, but their religion is simply a derivative of Paganism. If Paganism was taken away by a lesser form of Paganism, you still have a form of Paganism. It's hard for me to understand why God would assign a time-based prophecy to reveal when Paganism would be replaced by another form of Paganism.

3. 508 AD is seen as the beginning or the lead-off for the 1260-year prophecy that began in 538 AD. However, when have we seen any other prophecies in Daniel or Revelation requiring a lead-off? The 2300-day prophecy never required a soft starting point, then a hard starting point. The prophecy began when it began. The Bible told us that the Jews were given 70-weeks to get right with the Lord. We know that period began in 457 BC; however, would you believe me if I told you that there was a 30-year period before 457 BC that served as a lead-off for the greater 70-week timeframe? Wouldn't you be curious to understand why the 70-weeks prophecy required a 30-year "staging" period?

As much as I tried to make sense of the 508 AD soft starting point for the 1260-day prophecy, the more confused I became. I've conversed with people about the 508 AD starting point, but it felt like some individuals were so connected to that starting point that the mere suggestion of an alternative starting point was borderline heresy.

I believe the starting and ending points for the 2300-day and 1260-day prophecies are firm. There is no doubt in my mind that we have the correct timeframes for those prophecies. However, I didn't feel that the starting point for the 1290-day prophecy was on solid ground.

As I studied the Daily and the Abomination of Desolation, it became increasingly evident when the starting point for the 1290 days began. As a matter of fact, the starting point became so obvious that I was shocked I hadn't seen it before!

The 1290-Day prophecy revealed

Remember what Christ told Daniel? He said, "*And from the time that the daily sacrifice shall be taken away, and the abomination that maketh desolate set up, there shall be a thousand two hundred and ninety days.*"[29] The decline of Paganism is what enabled the Bishop of Rome to gain control over the Christian Church. Once Paganism was eliminated, the Roman Empire endowed the Bishop of Rome with Emperor-like powers, which enabled the transition from Christianity to Catholicism. The transition from Christianity to Catholicism is the focus of the Daily being taken away and the Abomination of Desolation being set up—and this transition took exactly 1290 years to occur!

They say Rome wasn't built in a day. While I agree with this expression, we must understand that even though Rome wasn't built in a day, it was founded on a day. According to tradition, Ancient Rome was founded by the two brothers, Romulus and Remus, on the 21st of April 753 BCE.[30] The fourth kingdom, which was prophesied to devour the whole earth, tread it down, and break it into pieces, began in 753 BC. Can you guess how long it took after 753 BC for the Christian Church to be given into the hands of the Roman Bishop? Exactly 1290 years!

---

[29] Daniel 12:11
[30] Mark, Joshua J.. "Ancient Rome." World History Encyclopedia. Last modified September 02, 2009. https://www.worldhistory.org/Rome/.

As I've told you before, I am not a mathematician. So in order to confirm this timeframe, I used a spreadsheet to count every year from 753 BC to 538 AD. According to my calculations, the 1290th year fell on 538 AD.[31] (See below)

	Year Beginning	Year Ending	Year Count
1			
2	-753	-752	1
3	-752	-751	2
4	-751	-750	3
1288	534	535	1287
1289	535	536	1288
1290	536	537	1289
1291	537	538	1290
1292	538	539	1291
1293			

Year 0 was removed.

Now, it's becoming clear what the 1290-year prophecy was conveying! Even though the Book of Daniel doesn't mention Rome by name, the 1290-year prophecy still identifies the Iron Empire by revealing the exact year Rome would be established and the exact year Rome would replace Christianity with Catholicism. While the 1260-day prophecy establishes the rise and fall of Papal Rome, the 1290-day prophecy establishes the rise and fall of Pagan Rome. Praise God for allowing us to see this truth!

---

[31] Year 0 was removed from the year begin and year end columns.

Now that we have established our starting and ending points for the 1290-day prophecy, our chart is almost complete. Let's see how this new information changes our chart:

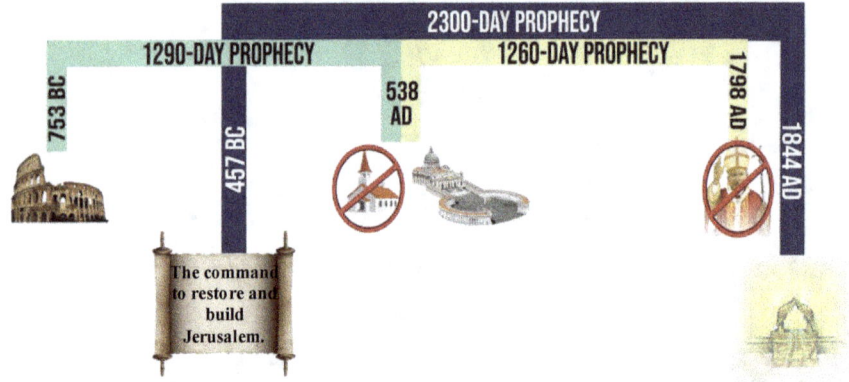

Chapter 7

The 1335-Day Prophecy

> *Blessed is he that waiteth, and cometh to the thousand three hundred and five and thirty days."* Daniel 12:12

Of all the time-based prophecies found in the Book of Daniel, I believe the 1335 days poses the biggest challenge. We aren't given a clear starting point, nor are we explicitly told how the fulfillment of this prophecy would be indicated. All we know is that those who wait and reach the 1335 days are blessed.

For months I searched for a revelation or clue as to the meaning of this 1335-day mystery, but unfortunately, I found none. Comparing history with prophecy produced no results. Every angle that I tried to approach this prophecy from resulted in the same conclusion—there simply isn't a period that matches up with this time-based prophecy. While I refuse to concoct the starting and ending points for the 1335 days using vague historical events, I also believe there's enough evidence to understand the intent of the 1335-day prophecy without those dates.

Excluding the 1335-day prophecy, Daniel established four prophetic timeframes: The 2300 days, the 70 weeks, the 1260 days, and the 1290 days.[32] To suggest that the 1335 days is independent of all the other time-based prophecies found in the Book of Daniel would be irresponsible of me. If Daniel had allocated more commentary detailing the 1335-day prophecy, then maybe an argument could be made that the start and end of the 1335 days stands independent of the other prophecies. However, with only one verse allocated to this prophecy, the 1335 days feels more like a footnote than a standalone prophecy. The brief reference made to the 1335 days is a strong indication that this time-based prophecy hinges on one of the other time-based prophecies established by Daniel. However, upon reviewing all the prophetic timeframes established by Daniel, I came to one conclusion regarding the 1335-day prophecy—it doesn't exist.

Before you throw this book in the trash, please allow me to clarify my statement. I'm not suggesting the 1335-day prophecy is a figment of our imagination, nor am I implying the Book of Daniel is dabbling in sleight of hand. What I am suggesting is that the prophetic timeframe originally mentioned in Daniel 12:12 was not 1335—it was 1305! Here I must warn you that I have no definitive proof that the original prophecy referenced 1305 days; I only have circumstantial evidence, which I will lay out. However, before we get into the evidence, you must understand what a copyist

---

[32] This excludes prophetic timeframes such as the 7 years Nebuchadnezzar was punished.

error is, and you also must understand that the Bible contains them.

Copyist errors

It's a well-known fact that the Bible is the best-selling book of all time. What enables the Bible to be a best seller is that copies of the Bible can easily be made from a printing press to meet the book's demand. However, before the printing press was invented, the only way to get a copy of the Bible was from a scribe, also known as a copyist. Please understand that there were no copy machines or scanners for these scribes, so the copies had to be handwritten. It should also be understood that these scribes were not inspired, and their work was unfortunately susceptible to errors. The errors are not attributed to the original manuscripts but rather the copies. The problem is, we don't have any of the original manuscripts. The Bibles that we read today are copies of a copy that, unfortunately, contains some copyist errors. I will not detail every copyist error in the Bible, but allow me to point out a few examples:

How long did Absalom wait?

> "And it came to pass after **forty years**, that Absalom said unto the king, I pray thee, let me go and pay my vow, which I have vowed unto the LORD, in Hebron."
> 2Samuel 15:7

It should be noted that Absalom could not have waited forty years as David's whole reign was forty years.³³ Most likely, the number should be four years which means the copyist accidentally changed this number.

How many stalls did Solomon own?

> And Solomon had **forty thousand stalls** of horses for his chariots, and twelve thousand horsemen. 1Kings 4:26

> And Solomon had **four thousand stalls** for horses and chariots, and twelve thousand horsemen; whom he bestowed in the chariot cities, and with the king at Jerusalem. 2Chronicles 9:25

Either Solomon had four thousand stalls or forty thousand stalls. In order to understand which number is correct, we find that 1Kings 10:26 reveals King Solomon had 1,400 chariots. It appears the forty thousand number is a copyist error, and the correct number should be four thousand.

When did Nebuzaradan come unto Jerusalem?

> "And in the **fifth month, on the seventh day** of the month, which is the nineteenth year of king Nebuchadnezzar king of Babylon, came Nebuzaradan, captain of the guard, a servant of the king of Babylon, unto Jerusalem." 2Kings 25:8

---
³³ 2 Samuel 5:4

> "Now in the **fifth month, in the tenth day of the month**, which was the nineteenth year of Nebuchadrezzar king of Babylon, came Nebuzaradan, captain of the guard, which served the king of Babylon, into Jerusalem." Jeremiah 52:12

It is possible that one account showed when Nebuchadnezzar arrived in Jerusalem, and the other account documented when he actually entered Jerusalem. However, it is likely that one of these accounts is simply a copyist error.

When was the head of Jehoiachin lifted up?

> "And it came to pass in the seven and thirtieth year of the captivity of Jehoiachin king of Judah, in the **twelfth month, on the seven and twentieth day of the month**, that Evilmerodach king of Babylon in the year that he began to reign did lift up the head of Jehoiachin king of Judah out of prison." 2Kings 25:27

> "And it came to pass in the seven and thirtieth year of the captivity of Jehoiachin king of Judah, in **the twelfth month, in the five and twentieth day of the month**, that Evilmerodach king of Babylon in the first year of his reign lifted up the head of Jehoiachin king of

Judah, and brought him forth out of prison." Jeremiah 52:31

Do you see the difference? Clearly, one of these timeframes is a copyist error.

I could continue, but I'm sure you get the point. The Bible contains a number of scribal errors. Some of these errors involve names and places, but many of them revolve around numbers.

But let me be clear; even with these errors, I maintain the belief that the Bible is still the inerrant Word of God. The Bible is *profitable for doctrine, for reproof, for correction,* and *for instruction in righteousness*[34]—and these are all free from error.

What I'm saying is that in many cases where the copyist made an error, we can still determine where the error is and what the correct wording should have been. In cases where we are not certain, it appears that these copyist errors are not contingent on Biblical doctrine. In other words, everything that is needed for salvation is free of copyist errors.

The 1335-day prophecy

Now that we understand what copyist errors are, allow me to clarify why I believe the 1335 days should be 1305 days.

As I previously mentioned, the 1335-day prophecy doesn't give us much explanation in order to determine if it's been fulfilled. All we know is that those who reach the 1335 days are blessed.

---

[34] 2Timothy 3:16

When looking at all of Daniel's time-based prophecies, we can only see a few scenarios where a blessing could come into play:

1. When the command to restore and build Jerusalem was given.
2. When Christ died for our sins towards the end of the 70-weeks prophecy.
3. At the end of the Papacy's reign in 1798 AD.
4. At the commencement of the Cleansing of the Sanctuary in 1844 AD.

If the blessing came at the command to build and restore Jerusalem, then the 1335-day prophecy would've reached its fulfillment in 457 BC. This means that the prophecy would have begun around 1792 BC. However, from my research, 1792 has no prophetic relevance, and thus we eliminate option one.

Had the 1335 days hinged on the Crucifixion of Christ, then Daniel 12 should have alluded to this event. Due to the fact Daniel 12 makes no references to the 70-weeks prophecy, we can also eliminate option two.

After 1798 AD, the Papacy received a deadly wound. Clearly, this was a blessing to those who suffered at the hands of the Roman Pontiff, but was this the fulfillment of the 1335-day prophecy? If the 1335 days ended in 1798 AD, then this means the prophecy would have begun around 463 AD. However, no event around that year pointed to the beginning of the prophecy, and there's nothing in Daniel 12 that would indicate that year being relevant. If we begin the 1335 days after 1798 AD, then this would take us past the year

1844 AD. It is unlikely that the 1335 days began after 1798 as we've already established there are no time prophecies after 1844. Considering the lack of a relevant date to correlate with 1798, we must eliminate option three as the fulfillment of the 1335-day prophecy.

1335 or 1305?

Eliminating options 1-3 leaves us with one last hope for understanding the 1335-day prophecy: Option four, which indicates this prophecy must relate to the Cleansing of the Sanctuary.

If you recall, we proved that the Cleansing of the Sanctuary was a work of judgment. This work is a blessing to those of us who are in Christ. The world may see believers as fanatics, as rigid, and in some cases anti-progressive to society. However, society is not our judge. God is the final judge, and even if the world shuns Christians, we are grateful that God doesn't use the world's standards for His final verdict. God's judgment is a blessing! If you don't believe me, then believe the Bible:

> And therefore will the LORD wait, that he may be gracious unto you, and therefore will he be exalted, that he may have mercy upon you: for **the LORD is a God of judgment: blessed are all they that wait for him.** Isaiah 30:18

According to Isaiah, there is a blessing for those who wait for the God of judgment. Now it makes sense why Jesus said, *Blessed is he that waiteth, and cometh to the thousand three hundred and five and thirty days.* God's judgment began at the end of this time-based prophecy! This reveals that the 1335 days extended to the year 1844 AD. However, this produces a problem. If 1844 fulfills the 1335-day prophecy, this will necessitate the prophecy beginning around 509 AD. Again, we see no reason to start this time-based prophecy in that year. So now the question is—When did the 1335-day prophecy begin? Well, if you recall, Daniel 12:11 also introduced us to the 1290-year prophecy. This prophecy began in 753 BC and ended in 538 AD.

Because the 1335-day prophecy was revealed immediately after the 1290-day prophecy, it is logical to assume the beginning of the 1335-day prophecy hinges on the ending of the 1290-day prophecy.

The mere suggestion that those who *wait* in order to come to the 1335 days suggests that we must *wait* until after the 1290 days have ended. Considering we don't have an exact date for the Papacy gaining supremacy, the 1335-day prophecy should begin after 538 AD. If we begin the 1335 days in 539 AD, it will take exactly 1,305 years to bring us to 1844!

Now do you understand why I believe 1335 was initially 1305? The prophecy known as the 1335-day prophecy *only* fits between the Daily-to-Abomination transition and the commencement of the Sanctuary being cleansed! This tells us that the 1335 days can only begin after 538 AD but must end before the close of 1844 AD! It is evident to me that the 1335-day prophecy is really a 1305-day prophecy.

Daniel 12 revealed that the Christian Church would be persecuted for 1260 years. Then this chapter revealed that this persecution would begin 1290 years from Rome's inception. And finally, God reminded Daniel that after the transition from Christianity to Roman Catholicism, there would be 1305 days remaining until the sanctuary would be cleansed.

The truth of "How Long"

Ladies and Gentlemen, you may not realize it, but the 1260, 1290, and 1335 day-prophecies are a response to the conversation in Daniel 8. If you remember, the angel asked this question:

> "...How long shall be the vision concerning the daily sacrifice, and the transgression of desolation, to give both the sanctuary and the host to be trodden under foot?" Daniel 8:13

Then this response was given:

> And he said unto me, Unto two thousand and three hundred days; then shall the sanctuary be cleansed. Daniel 8:14

We must understand these two verses contain three components that needed addressing:

1. How long until the vision concerning the Daily Sacrifice and the Abomination occurs?
2. How long will the sanctuary and the host be trodden under foot?
3. The Cleansing of the Sanctuary occurring at the end of the 2300 days.

You may not see it yet, but these three components found in Daniel 8 are addressed in Daniel 12.

- **Daniel 8 question** - "...How long shall be the vision concerning the **daily sacrifice, and the transgression of desolation?** Daniel 8:13
- **Daniel 12 answer** – "And from the time that the **daily sacrifice shall be taken away, and the abomination that maketh desolate set up**, there shall be a thousand two hundred and ninety days." Daniel 12:11

- **Daniel 8 question** - How long will **the sanctuary and the host** be permitted to be trodden underfoot?
- **Daniel 12 answer** – "...it shall be for a time, times, and an half; and when he shall have accomplished to **scatter the power of the holy people**..." Daniel 12:7

- **Daniel 8 declared when the Sanctuary would be cleansed** – "...Unto two thousand and three hundred days; then shall the sanctuary be cleansed." Daniel 8:14
- **Daniel 12 reveals when God's people would be blessed** – "Blessed is he that waiteth, and cometh to the thousand three hundred and five and thirty days." Daniel 12:12

It should be clear to you that Daniel 12 addressed all three components found in Daniel 8:13-14.

Now do you understand why the conversation between the angels was so important? The conversation in Daniel 8 helped us understand the conversation in Daniel 12—which ultimately gave us an understanding of the time-based prophecies in that chapter.

Considering my position on the 1335 days, it wouldn't shock me to know that some people may be skeptical—and I wouldn't blame them. It is also possible that some of you may be open to the idea that Daniel may have referred to 1305 days instead of 1335 days. Regardless of where you stand, this logical question may arise in your mind:

If 1335 is a copyist error, why didn't God simply prevent the copyist from mixing up the number?

This is a valid question and deserves some thought and attention. God is sovereign. He can control the winds and the rain and everything else under the sun. If God has control over everything, why didn't He ensure the copyist paid attention when Daniel 12:12 was copied? The answer is relatively simple. When we look at many of the copyist errors found in Scripture, it appears that God allowed minor human errors to be made by copyists when it referred to things such as names and numbers. However, even with these mishaps, we can still determine the content of the original manuscript by comparing many of these errors with other scriptures. So even though one copyist accidentally added a zero to the number of stalls Solomon owned, we have other scriptures to compare and decipher that Solomon only had 4,000 stalls instead of 40,000. The same concept applies to the 1335/1305-day prophecy. Just like we can compare two texts that refer to the same event and know which number is correct, we can also compare Daniel 12:12 with Daniel 8:14 and understand which prophecy contains the correct number of years. In essence, God allowed the 1335-day copyist mistake, knowing that the 2300-day prophecy found in Daniel 8 was enough to determine when the Sanctuary would be cleansed.

Could I be totally incorrect about the 1305-day prophecy? Absolutely! Because I only have circumstantial evidence that 1335 is a copyist error, it is possible that I am totally off-base in my assertion. However, you should know that I didn't come to this conclusion half-heartedly. My understanding of the 1305 day prophecy came through much prayer, fasting, and Bible study.

I am hopeful that one day we will stumble across an original manuscript of the Bible, which will either validate my position or prove me wrong. Whether my timeframes are correct or not, I think we can agree that the 1335 or 1305 days ended with the Cleansing of the Sanctuary, and thus we must remember that our focus should be on Christ. If Christ is in the process of Cleansing the Heavenly Sanctuary, and we not in Christ, then these time-based prophecies cannot help us. Now is the time to ask Jesus into your life. There is nothing from which God cannot save you. Trust in Him, obey His Word, and you will be saved.

I pray that this book has blessed someone who was previously confused about Daniel's time-based prophecies. You may not agree with everything I've written, but at least you now know *The Clear and Present Truth of the 2300, 1260, 1290, and 1335-day Prophecies.*

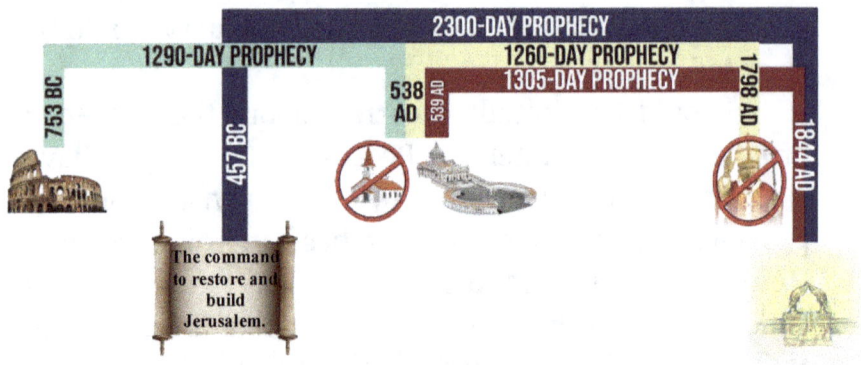

THE CLEAR AND PRESENT TRUTH OF THE 2300, 1260, 1290, AND 1335-DAY PROPHECIES

Test Your Knowledge

1. According to Ezekiel 4:6, a day in Bible prophecy is often calculated as a _____. (*p. 14*)

2. A year consisted of _____ days. (*p. 14*)

3. In BC, years are counted _____. (*p. 16*)

4. The sanctuary was God's method of dealing with the _____ of Israel. (*p. 25*)

5. Why did the sinner place his hands on the head of the sacrifice? (*pp. 26-27*)
   _____
   _____

6. Why did the priest carry the blood into the sanctuary? (*p. 28*)
   _____
   _____

7. Explain why the Sanctuary needed to be cleansed. (*pp. 28-29*)
   _____
   _____

8. How do we know the 70-weeks prophecy and the 2300-day prophecy began at the same time? (*pp. 32-33*)

_____
_____
_____
_____

9. When did the Cleansing of the Heavenly Sanctuary commence? (*p. 47*)

_____

10. What occurred during the 1260-day prophecy? (*pp. 71-72*)

_____
_____

11. What years marked the beginning and ending for the 1260-day prophecy? (*pp. 85-87*)

_____

12. Name a reason why 508 AD is an unlikely starting point for the 1290-day prophecy? (*pp. 106-107*)

_____
_____
_____
_____

13. What is the taking away of the Daily and the setting up of the Abomination of Desolation? (*pp. 101-104*)

14. What year did the Abomination of Desolation replace the Daily? (*p. 104*)

15. What is a copyist error? (*p. 113*)

16. What year was the 1335-day prophecy fulfilled? (*p. 119*)

Answers

1. According to Ezekiel 4:6, a day in Bible prophecy is often calculated as a **year**.

2. A year consisted of **360** days.

3. In BC, years are counted **backward**.

4. The sanctuary was God's method of dealing with the **sins** of Israel.

5. Why did the sinner place his hands on the head of the sacrifice? **The sinner symbolically transferred his sins to the animal.**

6. Why did the priest carry the blood into the sanctuary? **The priest symbolically transferred the sins to the sanctuary.**

7. Explain why the Sanctuary needed to be cleansed. **For a whole year, the sins of the people were transferred to the sanctuary. This necessitated a ceremony to remove those sins.**

8. How do we know the 70-weeks prophecy and the 2300 day prophecy began at the same time? **Daniel did not completely understand the vision of Daniel 8, and in Daniel 9, the angel came to give him understanding. Since no starting point was given for the 2300-day prophecy in Daniel 8, and the 70 weeks were declared to**

be cut out of another period, it's apparent the 70-weeks prophecy began simultaneously with the 2300-day prophecy.

9. When did the Cleansing of the Heavenly Sanctuary commence? **October 22, 1844**

10. What occurred during the 1260-day prophecy? **God's people suffered persecution.**

11. What years marked the start and end of the 1260-day prophecy? **538 AD - 1798 AD**

12. Name a reason why 508 AD is an unlikely starting point for the 1290-day prophecy?
If the 1290-day prophecy represented the supremacy of Catholicism over Paganism for 1290 years, there should've been a resurgence in Paganism at the close of the 1290-year prophecy.

13. What is the taking away of the Daily and the setting up of the Abomination of Desolation?
The Daily is the New Testament Church. The Abomination of Desolation represents the Roman Catholic Church. The taking away of the Daily and the setting up of the Abomination represents the Christian Church being replaced by the Roman Catholic Church.

14. What year did the Abomination of Desolation replace the Daily? **538 AD**

15. What is a copyist error? **A copyist error is a mistake made by the scribes when they made a copy of the scriptures.**

16. What year was the 1335-day prophecy fulfilled? **1844 AD**

Topical Index

1260-day prophecy, 12, 17, 67, 87, 106, 107
1290-day prophecy, 12, 17, 94, 98, 100, 105, 106, 107, 110
1335-day prophecy, 12, 17, 94, 111, 112, 116, 117, 118, 119
1798 AD, 87, 100, 106, 117
1844 AD, 36, 90, 117, 118, 119
2300-day prophecy, 12, 17, 21, 23, 33, 35, 36, 37, 43, 51, 55, 60, 64, 98, 107, 119, 120, 123
457 BC, 35, 37, 107, 117
508 AD, 98, 105, 107
538 AD, 85, 86, 100, 103, 104, 105, 106, 107, 109, 119
539 AD, 119
70-weeks prophecy, 33, 34, 35, 36, 107, 117
753 BC, 108, 109, 119
Abomination of Desolation, 21, 68, 98, 100, 101, 102, 103, 104, 105, 108
Antiochus Epiphanes, 60, 63, 101
Birth of Christ, 17
Bishop of Rome, 84, 104, 108
Catholicism, 100, 102, 103, 104, 105, 106, 108, 109, 120

Cleansing of the Sanctuary, 25, 29, 31, 35, 48, 54, 63, 89, 90, 117, 118, 120, 123
Copyist errors, 113
Daily Sacrifice, 19, 20, 21, 89, 90, 94, 98, 100, 101, 120
Day of Atonement, 29, 30, 38, 46, 47, 48, 49, 51, 52, 58, 59, 63
Day-for-a-year principle, 14
Earthly Sanctuary, 24, 43, 45, 46, 47, 51, 54, 55, 56, 58, 59, 60, 61, 72
France, 85
Heavenly Sanctuary, 42, 43, 45, 46, 47, 55, 56, 57, 58, 73, 74, 123
Holy City, 72, 73, 74, 103
Holy Place, 24, 28, 43, 45, 47, 48, 56, 57
Jerusalem, 34, 35, 37, 38, 72, 73, 103, 114, 115, 117
Judgment, 31, 48, 49, 50, 118, 119
Karaite Jews, 38
Kislev, 63
Most Holy Place, 24, 43, 47, 57
Paganism, 100, 101, 102, 103, 104, 105, 106, 108
Papacy, 80, 84, 85, 86, 87, 100, 105, 117, 119
Prophetic year, 14
Scapegoat, 30, 31, 51, 52, 53

Sin offering, 26, 27, 30, 44
Transgression of Desolation,
  19, 89, 90, 98

Two Witnesses, 66, 75, 78
Types and Shadows, 39, 40
Yom Kippur, 29, 38, 46, 49

www.ingramcontent.com/pod-product-compliance
Lightning Source LLC
Chambersburg PA
CBHW070913080526
44589CB00013B/1281